CITY AT

BY VICE ADMIRAL YOGI KAUFMAN

PHOTOGRAPHY BY STEVE AND YOGI KAUFMAN

FOREWORD BY ADMIRAL ARLEIGH BURKE

SEA

Naval Institute Press

Annapolis, Maryland

Library of Congress Cataloging-in-Publication Data

Kaufman, Yogi.
    City at sea / Yogi Kaufman ; photography
by Steve and Yogi Kaufman ; foreword by
Arleigh Burke.
        p.   cm.
    ISBN 1-55750-457-1 (alk. paper)
    1. Aircraft carriers–United States.
2. United States. Navy–Aviation. 3. United
States. Navy–Sea life. I. Title.
V874.3.K38   1995
359.9'435'0973–dc20   95-19081
Printed in the United States of America on
acid-free paper ⊗
02 01 00 99 98 97 96 95
9 8 7 6 5 4 3 2
First printing

PAGE I: AN F/A-18 HORNET CATA-PULTS OFF THE FLIGHT DECK OF THE USS *KITTY HAWK* AS AN F-14 TOMCAT IS MOVED INTO POSITION. PAGES II–III: THE USS *SARATOGA* CONDUCTS FLIGHT OPERATIONS IN THE ATLANTIC. *RIGHT:* AN F/A-18 HORNET LAUNCHES AT FULL POWER FROM THE CATAPULT OF THE USS *SARATOGA*. PAGES VI–VII: A PLANE CAPTAIN APPROACHES F/A-18 HORNETS ON THE FLIGHT DECK OF THE USS *KITTY HAWK* AT DAWN IN PREPARATION FOR MORNING FLIGHT OPERATIONS.

To Captain Dick Stolpe, close friend and fine naval aviator, who needled me for years with the thought that I should take time to learn something of the Navy other than the marvelous "fancy sewer pipes"—submarines—in which I had served my own naval career.

Dick, looking down on this confused world as you are, take comfort on several scores: to wit, that I have taken your advice; second, that the aviation navy is in good hands, perhaps even a tad better than a few decades back; and third, despite questioning looks by *modern* aviators, which attested to the antique nature of the garment, Steve kept your old flight suit "in commission" by wearing it during our photo flights!

To the entire community of carrier aviation—those who train, those who maintain and fix, those who fly, those who make the ships run, and, yes, those who wait for all these men and women.

And to Lucille—with whom the past half-century has been magic, but without whom it would have been empty of meaning for one husband and one son who love you always.

FOREWORD

I've never been an aviator, nor for most of my naval career did I have any background in aviation or aircraft carriers. I was and am a destroyerman, and by training and duty assignments an ordnance specialist—a member of the so-called "gun-club." In late 1943 and early 1944 I was in command of a magnificent destroyer squadron, DESRON 23, nicknamed the "Little Beavers." As far as a wartime assignment in the Navy goes, I was in heaven. These were true fighting ships, bristling with 5-inch and 40-mm guns, torpedo tubes, and racks of depth charges. Our hands were completely full with fighting the war against Japan in the South Pacific, and for most of us adrenalin replaced sleep. If a war had to be fought, there was no better place to be than where I was, carrying that war to the enemy in actions such as the Battles of Empress Augusta Bay and Cape St. George with battle-seasoned destroyers whose crews chomped at the bit to close the enemy at 31 knots—and more.

A bolt of lightning could not have given me a greater shock than the message orders I received detaching me immediately from DESRON 23 after only a short five months with that squadron. I was to report as chief of staff to Commander, Carrier Division 3! I was astonished, to put it mildly. A destroyerman—a non-aviator—fighting a war in a massive ship manned by thousands and armed with scores of airplanes! This was almost beyond my comprehension. I recall writing to an old friend that I was at a loss to explain my orders, that they were so sudden and it was so late in the game that there was nothing I could do about them, that this was neither a job that I would like nor for which I was fitted—but maybe it would be good for my soul.

The date 27 March 1944 found our squadron in rendezvous with the Fifth Fleet, and I was transferred in the fashion appropriate for seagoing sailors—by high line—from my flagship, the destroyer *Ausburne,* to the new carrier *Lexington,* flagship of Vice Admiral Marc A. "Pete" Mitscher. Mitscher had just been promoted to three stars and

FACING PAGE, VICE ADMIRAL MARC A. MITSCHER AND THEN-CAPTAIN ARLEIGH A. BURKE, HIS CHIEF OF STAFF, PLAN STRIKE OPERATIONS ABOARD HIS FLAGSHIP IN THE SOUTH PACIFIC DURING WORLD WAR II. (COURTESY OF MRS. MARC A. MITSCHER)

PREVIOUS PAGE, THE NUCLEAR AIRCRAFT CARRIER USS *GEORGE WASHINGTON* PREPARES FOR FLIGHT OPERATIONS OFF PUERTO RICO.

fleeted up to Commander, Fast Carrier Task Forces Pacific. I reported to him in his usual spot on the flag bridge as he sat in his swivel chair, facing aft—as he would say, "only a damned fool would ride with the wind in his face!" My crash course in aircraft carriers, the world of airplanes, and the tactics of large forces of fighters, dive-bombers, and torpedo planes had begun. Within days I was to be completely caught up in a new phase of fighting—great numbers of ships facing similar enemy forces, but with the star players now in this later stage of war being aircraft carriers and their aircraft.

I had to learn fast—very fast. Mitscher's huge Task Force 58, made up of seventy-eight ships, was steaming in several circular formations toward the Palau Islands to attack three days later. I quizzed every person I encountered on the bridge and in the operating spaces, read operation orders and every manual I could get my hands on that had to do with my job. On my second night aboard, the Japanese planes attacked, and our ships countered in a hellish display of firepower. The next day I was on the flag bridge as torpedo planes attacked, heading directly for our ships in daylight, and I reacted by giving orders on the TBS radio; that, as it turned out, was quite unnecessary—our battle-seasoned ships had already taken the necessary action, turning toward the attackers—standard operating procedure for these big ships, same as it had been in my destroyers!

With such a high tempo of combat, it took very little time for me to learn the "ins and outs" of carrier operations and tactics in coordination of large fleets. It's hard to imagine today—Mitscher's force included up to fifteen carriers at times! I've heard educators refer to situations like mine as "total immersion"—very conducive to rapid and thorough learning. Within days I became fairly comfortable both with my role in giving orders in Mitscher's name, but also with the canny admiral himself. And seeing them fighting the enemy on a daily basis, I gained increasing admiration for the pilots and their ability and endurance in bringing our airplanes back, turning them around, and returning to shoot down enemy planes or to bomb or torpedo their bases or ships. At this stage of the war, their thorough training proved a marked advantage over the lesser-trained Japanese pilots, whose experience levels dropped rapidly as our forces shot down large numbers in every action. In the famed "Marianas Turkey Shoot" of June 1944, for example, during the Battle of the Philippine Sea, our forces shot down thirteen enemy for each of our losses! Tremendous attrition!

Less noticed than the pilots, but as essential and maybe even more tireless, were the scores of very young bluejackets who made up the flight-deck and hangar-deck crews, doing jobs that were decidedly hazardous, but especially so when one was tired or lacking sleep. Their working hours continued even as the pilots slept, what with patching up damaged planes, loading ammunition, and performing routine maintenance. Somehow they would manage to grab a bite to eat and perhaps nap atop an ammunition locker or under the wing of a plane. Their performance was matched by the engineering and damage-control people, the medics, the cooks—the entire crews. These people—all of them, from seamen to captains—were not just good, they were great! Of course, that's why we won.

Increasingly fast paced action brought the war in the Pacific into its final phases as we fought the Battle for Leyte Gulf, made strikes on Japan, and withstood the onslaught of kamikaze suicide planes during the campaigns for Iwo Jima and Okinawa. We lost ships, and heroism was the order of the day in many quarters, such as the great human efforts that prevented the sinking of the *Franklin* despite terrible damage and loss of life. Two attacking aircraft hit our flagship, the *Bunker Hill,* causing severe damage and forcing the transfer of Mitscher and our staff to the *Enterprise.* Then this new flagship was hit by a kamikaze. The fires and damage caused yet another shift of the remaining staff to the *Randolph*—and that ship had just been patched up from an earlier kamikaze hit! These were tough times, and it took tough men and tough ships to do the job. The ability of those carriers to suffer almost lethal damage, yet return to fight, was key to assuring the air power that was essential to our victory in the Pacific. The carrier was here to stay—no doubt about it!

My battle experience with the carriers was invaluable as I continued my career. There simply is no substitute for carrier air power in the modern scheme of war, and as the Chief of Naval Operations I campaigned for funding to build nuclear carriers, which were to prove even more capable than those fine ships I had known. Our modern carriers are difficult to categorize as mere ships—they're huge, as befits a ship that must carry meaningful numbers of airplanes with different missions and capabilities, each of which adds vital parts to the whole force. Some claim that these modern carriers are built so that they won't sink. I hope that their very presence is enough to deter the only means of finding out. I'm told that our young pilots are brighter, better trained, more confident, and more experienced than ever—tremendous accolades when compared with the accomplishments of their predecessors! They and the great ships that carry them—virtual cities of steel, cities at sea—are proving their value repeatedly in carrying out national policy in a changing world.

The photographer-authors of this book pay tribute to these fine young warriors and to the magnificent carriers, as do I. However, they go further by placing the primary focus of their photographic tribute on the bluejackets and the ships, a thrust that I find refreshing and commend to your viewing—for behind those superb pilots on every ship are 5,500 largely unsung Navy men who wear blue or khaki and truly, in carriers, the colors of the rainbow. They are "the butcher, the baker, the candlestick maker" of the city at sea, without whom the most proficient captains or pilots would find it impossible to carry out the real function of the carrier and its airplanes: placing ordnance on target!

Arleigh Burke

THE PILOT OF AN F/A-18 HORNET STRAPS IN

JUST PRIOR TO CATAPULTING OFF FROM THE

KITTY HAWK.

PREFACE

One cannot be on a modern aircraft carrier many minutes without realizing that this floating marvel is indeed a "city at sea." True, this ship and the barely two handfuls like it are, by population, very small cities, but they respond almost daily to situations that test the highest national leadership in its conduct of national resolve and policy. Any one of these small cities may at any given time become the most important in the world!

Even at its quietest time, when not involved in launching or recovering its "main battery"—scores of naval aircraft—a carrier remains a beehive of activity. The two-hundred-plus pilots and flight officers might find time for much-needed rest when the activity directly related to flight operations ceases, but the bustling goes on. A large percentage of the population of some five thousand to six thousand is always busy. Sailors work through the night, performing myriad maintenance and testing procedures on aircraft and support equipment, while others operate radars and radio equipment to assure safe passage through waters placid or hostile. Some operate the power plants that provide electrical power and propulsion, or plan the details of future operations that may include strikes on targets, intelligence gathering, or realistic exercises with other ships and aircraft.

Many decks below, in the bowels of the ship, weapons personnel carefully—very carefully—assemble bombs or missiles. Cooks cook, bakers bake, catapult personnel test catapults—a procedure not conducive to restful sleep—and yes, some sleep, though such seems almost a luxury for much of the time at sea. The pace of work continues for hundreds—officers, chief petty officers, petty officers, airmen, seamen, firemen, and marines—whose entire purpose lies in contributing to the optimum performance of the airplanes and their pilots. These are "the butchers, the bakers, the candlestick makers" of this "city at sea." They make it work.

This book is a photographic testimony to the superb job performed on a daily basis by the community of naval aviation and is not intended as an historical account of the aircraft carrier's evolution. We should, though, ponder for a moment the character of this great and mighty weapons system. With the development and maturing of the large carriers in World War II, the age of the battleship as the fleet's stalwart became history, as, indeed, did the large guns themselves. The mobility of fast carrier task forces, whose aircraft were capable of striking and destroying the enemy hundreds of miles away, became an overpowering force and changed the nature of war decisively.

One might have believed that the lessons of the long and hard-fought World War II would have been so indelibly inscribed in the memories of American leaders as to assure a thriving Navy immune to slashing, emasculating budgetary measures. That would be flying in the face of history! Reduce—cut back—mothball—decommission—stop building—butter, not guns—too many—too large—too expensive: the same themes, again, that had resulted in the shell of a Navy of the 1930s! There come to mind several lines from a memorable poem "Old Ironsides," written by Oliver Wendell Holmes in 1830 in indignant protest against the condemnation and destruction of the frigate *Constitution*:

> No more shall feel the victor's tread,
> Or know the conquered knee;
> The harpies of the shore shall pluck
> The eagle from the sea!

The "harpies" tried, as they do today, but didn't prevail. True—gone are the days when a major U.S. fleet in battle might bring fifteen carriers to bear in one part of an ocean, but hard-fought bureaucratic battles resulted in retaining a meaningful force of large carriers, and in laying the groundwork for better to come. Some of the toughest battles of the 1950s into the 1970s were fought against a combative establishment aligned against the Navy, employing systems analysts often much more enamored with studying the problem than finding a solution. Size was a concept that seemed to elude their grasp, as was the added tactical value of nuclear power versus its expense. Many, including at times some senior non-aviator admirals, failed to understand the synergism available only to a carrier large enough to carry adequate numbers of each different type of aircraft needed to produce a "critical mass" within an air wing—sustainable numbers of reconnaissance, electronic jamming, antisubmarine, command-and-control, and tanker aircraft and helicopters to support and direct flights of fighters and bombers.

The emergence of the Soviet Navy as a blue-water contestant, bristling with nuclear submarines and a fleet of missile-carrying ships—coupled with the fear of nuclear-weapons exchanges at sea—

fueled the criticism by many, including members of Congress, that carriers were too vulnerable, too large, or too expensive. Nuclear-powered carriers in particular drew the wrath and venom of those "bean counters" who attempted to show that three smaller conventionally powered carriers could be bought for the price of two nuclear ships. Again and again Navy studies were cited to show that it would take two of the lesser ships to equal the performance of the larger ship.

The effectiveness of the first nuclear carrier, the USS *Enterprise,* in producing very high sortie rates in Vietnam provided a valuable selling point. Still, critics used terms like "dinosaurs" or "sitting ducks," and naval leaders—from the earliest days of Admiral Arleigh Burke's tenure as CNO, right up to the present—have had to recite past lessons learned to build backfires against budgetary attacks. Where reason alone could not be counted on to cut the mustard, a succession of great leaders as chiefs of naval operations, assisted mightily in their drive for nuclear propulsion by Admiral Hyman Rickover and his successors, have successfully employed the tactics of persuasion, repetition, abrasion, percussion, and perhaps osmosis to defeat hard-set opposition and gain recognition of the Navy's need for a force of modern carriers that can meet the requirements of national policy.

Washington's shenanigans, though, escape the notice of the very active carrier crews as they go about their daily business. Such lofty subjects are simply "not their circuit." The top echelons of command, especially the more senior officers who have spent a duty tour in Washington, will of course track the progress of shipbuilding and decommissioning programs—such is their lifeblood. But those who slug it out daily on the deck plates and in the furious pace of flight operations are much too engrossed in flying, caring for aircraft, operating machinery, maintenance, cooking, cleaning, and trying to get enough rest to start all over again to worry too much about such policy matters. Tomorrow may bring an uneventful day, perhaps a Sunday with minimal flight ops—or it could bring a Suez Canal transit, a repeat of one made only days earlier when in a "yo-yo" transit sequence of "the ditch" a very busy carrier responds to the latest Bosnian burp or Mideast mishap. Sailors in jerseys of hues of the rainbow accept the challenge, shrug, "Whatever!," smile, and take on the changed assignment with fantastic spirit and youthful enthusiasm. They can handle it.

There are marvelous books portraying the beauty of flight and featuring closeups of pilots flying their wondrous machines in aerial maneuvers and formations. Their photographs are breathtakingly beautiful and defy improvement. In this book the photographer-authors make no attempt to challenge the air-to-air wizards who have produced such beauty. The aircraft, especially those flown from carriers, are technological wonders, and the pilots who fly them and land on so tiny a piece of real estate surrounded by hostile seas earn the gratitude of a nation, as do the photographers who have captured them for all in their finest moments—in flight. In approaching this book, the authors were struck by the story of the totality of carrier operations and opted to place primary focus upon sailors and the ship, with individual crew members describing their duties in interviews. Recognizing that the spirit and machismo, the ever-present "can do" attitude inherent in naval aviation, actually has its foundation in the far-reaching and eminently successful training program, enough of the training sites were photographed to set the tone for later at-sea operations. Aviation training by itself could fill several books! Later, many days on carriers at sea, in port, and even in dry dock produced the photographs included in this book to depict life on board the carrier, the stress of flight operations, and the homecoming following a six-month deployment. Throughout, the authors were provided proof that naval aviation exudes a very positive attitude. Repeatedly, when a challenge was posed, the same words were heard that were heard in the first visits to a training squadron—"We can make it work!" In this busy community, the sometimes too-ready "can do" gives way to "will do," and in most difficult situations to "have done!"

OPPOSITE, **AN AIR CONTROLLER ON BOARD A CARRIER DIRECTS AIR TRAFFIC AROUND THE SHIP IN A SIMILAR MANNER TO AIR CONTROLLERS AT BUSY AIRPORTS OF LARGE CITIES.**

FOLLOWING PAGE, **A DECK-EDGE OPERATOR SIGNALS AS HE FIRES THE CATAPULT.**

BELOW, **THE BRIDGE WATCH ON BOARD THE USS** *KITTY HAWK* **IN THE PACIFIC. A WATCH STANDER WRITES INFORMATION ON RADAR CONTACTS BACKWARD TO BE READ FROM THE OPPOSITE SIDE OF THE STATUS BOARD BY THE CAPTAIN AND BRIDGE PERSONNEL.**

ACKNOWLEDGMENTS

The few words we offer here only scratch the surface in expressing our deep and sincere appreciation for the patience, understanding, cooperation, and infectious enthusiasm of the men and women—uniformed and civilian—of the U.S. Navy, the various training commands, and in particular the Naval Air Forces Atlantic and Pacific. We are grateful for the encouragement and especially for the access provided at the outset of our endeavors by the Chief of Naval Operations, Admiral Frank Kelso—which continued under his successor, Admiral Mike Boorda—as well as to the director of nuclear propulsion, Admiral Bruce DeMars.

The efficient organization of old friend Vice Admiral Bob Kihunc ensured that we got a thorough look at the aviation training commands and the unsung heroes of that environment. Our tours aboard carriers were thoughtfully arranged by the force commanders, Vice Admirals Tony Less and Rocky Spane. They placed us on the *Saratoga*, *Kitty Hawk*, and *George Washington*, where we were educated and dazzled by crews led by Captains Don Weiss, Bill "Bear" Pickavance, and Bob Sprigg. Aboard *Saratoga* an E2C controller, Lieutenant Commander Tom Jarrell, put on a bravura performance in giving us our initial carrier and aviation indoctrination for four nonstop days. You guys and your people were superb! We only hope that we do you justice.

To Chief of Information Rear Admiral Kendell Pease, our sincerest thanks for the outstanding efforts of a talented and energetic public affairs office. Particular credit goes to Commanders Kevin Wensing and Joe March; Lieutenant Commanders Jack Papp and John Brindley; Lieutenants Matt Brown, Rob Newell, Beth Jones, and Ken Ross; Senior Chief Petty Officer Pat Neal; and Michelle Harrison.

We are indebted to our colleague in England, John Batchelor, for his superb talents and for allowing us to use his fine graphic of a *Nimitz*-class aircraft carrier.

We are grateful for the efforts and encouragement of the Naval Institute Press staff throughout the publishing process. Finally, we join the Naval Institute Foundation in recognizing generous grants from Bozell Worldwide Inc., the Martin Marietta Corporation, McDonnell Douglas Aerospace, and the Northrop Grumman Corporation, without which this book might not have been possible.

PREVIOUS PAGES, IN A FINAL CHECKOUT OF HIS

F-14 TOMCAT, A RADAR INTERCEPT OFFICER

INSPECTS WING AND FIXTURES PRIOR TO TAKE-

OFF FROM *KITTY HAWK.* HELICOPTER VIEW OF

A PORTION OF THE "MAIN BATTERY"—ITS AIR

WING—OF THE USS *GEORGE WASHINGTON.*

ABOVE, COLORFUL SUNSET REFLECTS OFF

AIRCRAFT ON USS *KITTY HAWK'S* FLIGHT

DECK.

OPPOSITE, AN F-14 TOMCAT MOVES INTO

LAUNCH POSITION.

TRAINING

Pensacola. They call it "the cradle of naval aviation," and it doesn't take long for a visitor to understand why. All flight training begins at Naval Air Station, Pensacola, Florida, as it has for most naval aviators, past or present. Old-timers who had worn or still wear wings of gold had convinced the authors that a "swing" through the pilot-training complex was essential to gaining an appreciation for the urgency, spirit, and enthusiasm to be recorded on board aircraft carriers. They were right. The crews of carriers, the procedures, the religious adherence to the tenets of safety or double-checking, a "can do" will, the ship itself—all work to assure the success of the actually small number who are the pilots or crews of the carrier's aircraft. The enthusiasm and bravado that mark everything they do from the earliest days of their flight training is passed to the ships' crews and air wing personnel. Their effectiveness results from the efforts of thousands—officer, enlisted, and civilian—starting with the recruit commands and extending to the whole of the aviation-training complex. This is where it starts—the feeling of ownership and investment by all in the abilities of the young men and women who fly those powerful aircraft from the decks of the carriers. To use an overworked but true cliché, all march to the drumbeat of the pilots!

During our first visit to Pensacola, two things very graphically were impressed upon the mind. First, at the airport itself, a magnificent display of a Grumman F-11F Tiger—adorned in the colors of the Blue Angels demonstration flying team—attested to the city's place as "home of the Blue Angels." Next, a huge billboard proudly proclaimed, "Pensacola—Birthplace of Emmitt Smith!" The Dallas Cowboy Super Bowl superhero and his prowess aren't lost on his hometown, nor is naval aviation. Looking at a water tank on most air bases, a visitor "gets

OPPOSITE, **THE WATER TOWER AT THE CORPUS CHRISTI BASE ADVERTISES THE BUSINESS AT HAND.**

the word"—"Fly Navy." One need only look at the license plates and bumper stickers of the cars at the base exchanges or officers quarters. No bashfulness here! But who would want it otherwise?

Pensacola is the first stop for naval aviators and naval flight officers, and for many it will be their final home upon retiring after a twenty-to-thirty-or-so year career. Loyalty to the cult that wears the wings of gold continues long after one has grown too long in the tooth to fly, and this loyalty and active promotion of naval aviation as "the only way to go" goes a long way in assuring a healthy and continuing influx of recruits. Scores of officers and petty officers migrate back to the scene of their aviation "roots," some to happily while away the years golfing and enjoying, finally, a quiet life among lifetime friends—for others, to continue actively and aggressively promoting naval aviation and inspiring hundreds of future aviators by leading and serving programs such as the Navy League or the world-class National Museum of Naval Aviation.

Watch as a horde of eleven-to-fourteen-year-old red-blooded Boy Scouts descends upon the museum! They are greeted and led by a docent, usually a retired naval aviator and proud of it—one of upward of 250 whose loyalty to naval aviation remains unswerving to the grave and who volunteer their time to show off the superb museum. At the same time, they will regale visitors with personal vignettes from their own action-filled careers. The spirit is so positive that it can almost be cut with a knife and served to the youngsters, who find it infectious. One look at the towering central display of a wing-on-wing formation of four Blue Angels' aircraft from a bygone day—displayed so realistically that the only thing missing is the roar of the jets—and even the shyest of the group is hooked. And if a combination of scores of action-filled movies of the ilk of *Top Gun* and static displays such as the museum's don't create enough interest, the aviators here can bring to bear their "secret weapon"—an "unfair advantage" as seen by surface-ship and submarine recruiters—the Navy's Blue Angels! Flying what many pilots today call "the airplane of choice"—the new F/A-18 Hornets—the team tours the United States, dazzling excited audiences in more than fifty air shows annually. Little wonder that pilot training continues to attract the brightest and best!

Young men and women with wings in their eyes report to Pensacola from the U.S. Naval Academy, various university Naval ROTC units, and Aviation Officer Candidate School. Dependent upon the source, they first undergo from six to fourteen weeks of tough preflight indoctrination—academics, military drill, stress training, physical fitness, lots of swimming, and a unique water-survival course. None will forget the first experience in the "dunker" as they escape from a simulated but very realistic aircraft that is "crashed" and inverted underwater, nor their final escape—blindfolded. Aviation physiology programs give them a taste of the woozy effects of oxygen deprivation at high altitudes and the jolt of ejecting from an aircraft, while a devilish whirling-dervish of a machine defies their equilibrium or probes the sensitivity and queasiness of their stomachs.

Preflight over, they get to fly! The next hurdle is Primary Training. Some report to Whiting Field, near Pensacola, while others begin their flying at Naval Air Station, Corpus Christi, Texas. Naval flight officers remain in Pensacola and receive their first flight instruction in the same model of training airplanes as the pilots. As one moves about the Navy's training bases, the enormity of the program sinks in. The Training Command has five training air wings located on five air stations in Florida, Mississippi, and Texas, and employs more than eleven thousand military and civilian naval personnel and civilian contractors. Included are 900 instructor pilots and 850 aircraft that fly 400,000 hours annually in cranking out 1,250 pilots and 400 naval flight officers. The bases are huge, carved out of sandy fields or scrub-pine thickets, and they're flat—so flat one can imagine the earth's curvature at the visible horizon. For most of the year they are hot and humid, surely selected to add spice to the stress of a pilot confined to a hot airplane. For an East-Coaster, even the language of the regions takes a little time to learn. On the Gulf Coast, we had to decipher what the "fants" are that we were supposed to watch out for—fire ants. Or while catching a sunrise breakfast at McDonald's en route to Naval Air Station, Kingsville, we noted that the dulcet voices of the entire clientele were speaking Spanish. The outlying bases seem swallowed up by the vastness of the flat plains, and traffic on the highways doesn't seem a problem. But a truism—the base is the biggest thing in town!

Twenty-two weeks of Primary Training include sixty-seven hours of flight in a Beechcraft T-34C Mentor, a turbo-prop model that is fully aerobatic. After thirteen flights, students "solo," and those succeeding are treated to the traditional necktie-cutting ceremony, a fun-filled though brief pause in this phase, which also includes twenty-seven hours of simulator training plus almost two hundred hours of academics. This amounts to the "playoffs" for the budding pilots. The pipeline they will now follow depends largely upon their demonstrated abilities during Primary, with fleet requirements and their own preferences playing a part. Jet (strike) training is the most sought after of the four pipelines—not surprising, given the extroverted nature of most student pilots. However, talking with those who advance to the other pipelines—multi-engine, E-2/C-2 reconnaissance or carrier support, or helicopter—reveals that aside from early disappointment for some, most settle down to serious work, whichever route is theirs. The driving desire is to fly—in anything.

Students selected for strike—carrier-based jet aviation—move to Kingsville, Texas, or Meridian, Mississippi, for jet training. There, in the twenty-three-week Intermediate Phase of jet training, they fly the T-2C Buckeye, concentrating on formation flying, air-to-air gunnery, and advanced instrument flying and getting their first opportunity to experience the gut-wrenching carrier landing, also called a "trap"! If successful, they will make four carrier landings and, of course, will be catapulted off.

They will then move to a twenty-five-week Advanced Phase, flying the TA-4J Skyhawk, a two-seat trainer model of the light-attack airplane used during the Vietnam War. Commencing in 1994, the Navy has begun to phase in a revolutionary training system, the integrated T-45 Goshawk training system, with state-of-the-art simulators and the Goshawk aircraft, which supplants both earlier jet trainers. At this point students learn tactics, drop practice bombs, shoot missiles, perform gunnery runs against land targets, and move into dogfighting. Six more arrested landings will then be made on a carrier, after which they will be treated to a "winging" ceremony, a celebratory occasion at which their gold wings will be pinned on. In all, jet pilots will have undergone from seventy-six to eighty-four weeks of intensive and rigorous academics and theory, survival training, physical conditioning, and flying—including ten arrested carrier landings, an event they will never take for granted, especially at night! Other pilot pipelines feature similar challenging paths, although they are not quite so long as the jet program.

Naval flight officers (NFOs)—some laughingly call themselves "the thinking-man's aviator"—serve vital roles as weapons-systems operators, tactical coordinators, navigators, or electronic-warfare or intercept officers. The curricula for NFOs are as intensive as for pilots—some may say more so. Student NFOs find themselves learning to navigate with radar while whizzing at 420 knots at high altitude or at 300 knots while seeing the ground pass by only 500 feet below. Some will memorize the intricate parameters of threat sensors, master the most effective tactics for delivering weapons against air or land targets, or become expert at controlling the air-to-air battle. Ultimately, it's the NFOs who detect and report enemy contacts, coordinate the attack by friendly aircraft, and in short—in the words of one skilled mission commander of an E-2C Hawkeye—"We keep the admiral out of trouble!"

A "DEVIL'S CONTRAPTION" TESTS THE
EQUILIBRIUM OF STUDENT AVIATORS AND
TEACHES RELIANCE UPON INSTRUMENTS
RATHER THAN ON INDIVIDUAL PERCEPTION
OF ATTITUDE. EACH SMALLER MODULE
CONTAINS A STUDENT AND SPINS INDEPEN-
DENTLY OF THE MAIN FRAME, WHICH IS
ITSELF SPINNING AT VARIABLE SPEEDS.

OPPOSITE, AT PENSACOLA, HELICOPTER RESCUE CREWS RECEIVE ARDUOUS WATER TRAINING AND ADVANCED SWIMMING TO DEVELOP THE SKILLS NECESSARY TO RES-CUE DOWNED AVIATORS AT SEA.

RIGHT, AT NAVAL AIR STATION, PENSACOLA, STUDENTS RECEIVE FIRST-HAND INDOCTRINATION IN THE IMPACT OF EJECTION FROM AN AIRCRAFT BY MEANS OF A SIMULATOR THAT DUPLICATES THE FORCES OF AN EMERGENCY EGRESS.

BELOW, A WOMAN STUDENT PILOT AT PENSACOLA RECEIVES EARLY INDOCTRINATION AND SKILL DEVELOP-MENT IN SIMPLE SIMULATOR-TRAINING AIDS UNDER THE HELPFUL AND WATCHFUL EYES OF AN INSTRUCTOR PILOT.

ABOVE, NAVAL AIR STATION, KINGSVILLE, TEXAS, PROVIDES FACILITIES FOR ADVANCED HELICOPTER TRAINING USING JET RANGER AIRCRAFT AND ADVANCED SIMULATORS.

PREVIOUS PAGE, A LINEUP OF T-34 TRAINING AIRCRAFT GIVES A CLUE TO SIZE OF THE FLIGHT-TRAINING ESTABLISHMENT IN THE STATES OF FLORIDA, TEXAS, AND MISSISSIPPI. THE T-34 PROPELLER AIRCRAFT PROVIDES INITIAL FLIGHT TRAINING FOR AVIATORS.

ABOVE, AT PENSACOLA, STUDENT PILOTS LEARN EARLY

IN THEIR FLIGHT TRAINING THAT THEY ARE PERSONALLY

RESPONSIBLE FOR CHECKING THEIR AIRCRAFT AND ITS

EQUIPMENT FOR FLIGHT-WORTHINESS.

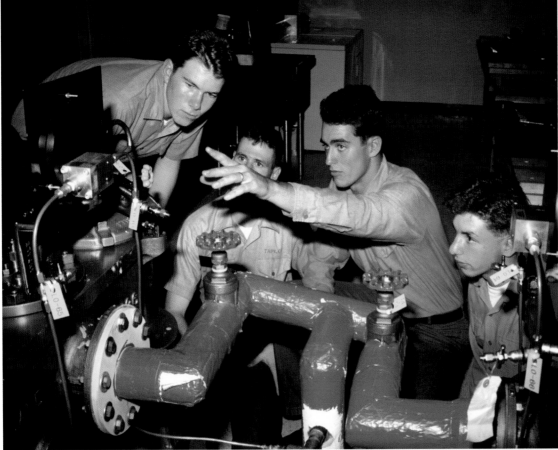

ABOVE, ENLISTED CREW MEMBERS OF CARRIERS RECEIVE
BASIC AND ADVANCED SKILL TRAINING IN THEIR SPECIAL-
TIES FOR MONTHS PRIOR TO REPORTING TO A SHIP. HERE,
STUDENTS IN THE NUCLEAR FIELD CLASS "A" SCHOOL
LEARN THE RUDIMENTS OF A LUBRICATING-OIL SYSTEM.

OPPOSITE, IN DAMAGE-CONTROL TRAINING AT NAVAL
BASE, NORFOLK, VIRGINIA, TEAMS FROM INDIVIDUAL
SHIPS ARE GIVEN REALISTIC EXPERIENCE IN CONTROLLING
BURST PIPES, FLOODED COMPARTMENTS, AND HULL
DAMAGE, IN SOME CASES BEING FORCED TO COMPLETE
THE EXERCISE AS WATER RISES ABOVE THEIR HEADS.

RIGHT, FIRE-FIGHTING TRAINING ASHORE AT NAVAL BASE,
NORFOLK, AND AT EVEN MORE ADVANCED TRAINERS AT
OTHER SITES PROVIDES TEAMS FROM SHIPS WITH THE
EXPERIENCE AND SKILL TO COMBAT THE FIERCE FIRES
THAT MAY ACCOMPANY AIR OPERATIONS AND BATTLE
DAMAGE.

AFTER A NUMBER OF INDOCTRINATION FLIGHTS WITH AN INSTRUCTOR, STUDENT PILOTS SOLO. SUCCESS SUBJECTS THEM TO THE TRADITIONAL CEREMONY IN WHICH INSTRUCTORS CUT OFF THEIR STUDENTS' NECKTIES.

A WOMAN STUDENT PILOT PREPARES FOR TAKEOFF IN A T-2 BUCKEYE JET TRAINER UNDER THE WATCHFUL EYE OF AN INSTRUC-TOR AT NAVAL AIR STATION, KINGSVILLE, TEXAS.

TRAINING WING COMMANDER

We're taking young people who have never had a thing to do with a high-stress situation and trying to turn them into combat-proficient pilots—there's a massive change that occurs there as we bring pressure to bear, lots of pressure. The route is all graded, and graded hard, and each guy or woman knows that. There's no slack and no "easy day," and the pressure is constant because they know the better they do on the grades, the better their chances are of getting their first choice of air-plane type. At this point in training, all the students know is that they're going to be pilots—they don't start out being funneled into one type or another. There's supposed to be a fair sharing between the various aircraft-type communities on getting top performers, but the universal truth is that those who do the best are going to have a lot bet-ter shot at getting the kind of plane they want to fly in for a Navy career.

The personalities that venture into this arena are not timid. When they walk in the door, they very quickly figure out where they want to wind up, and they start going for that. The stresses that we see, the physical stresses, start building up early and are clearly evident. They show up in the simple act of strapping into an airplane on a hot day—and, God, someone years ago must have picked this hot, flat Texas area to build up the stress and sweat—but the stress of doing just that when they're about to do something for the first time—say it's the first time they're going to spin an airplane or engage in air combat maneuver-ing—or the first time they go out and bomb—or they're on a check ride—high stress from a performance point of view. Before they ever sit down in the airplane they'll be a ball of sweat. Picture them sitting in the pilot's seat, and they'll be wiping sweat out of their eyes as they're trying to strap down.

The instructor, who's been doing this for quite a while, knows what's coming and is calm, but the student in the hot seat, for perfor-mance, is really pumped up. I remember particularly well my first time at air combat maneuvering—a three-dimensional thing—it's you against the other guy. He's gonna know whether you're doing it right or not, or whether you win. This is not a simple academic training thing. Not too far in the future, being good at that can mean whether you live or die. The first time you engage, you meet your opponent head-on, and at the pass you start to turn the airplane hard. All that sweat that you've been pouring out of your head over the last twenty minutes has been soaking up in the sponge-rubber pads of your hel-met, and as you start pulling 6 Gs in the turn, the helmet is squashed down on your head and squeezes out all that sweat, and it just pours down over your eyes and face! I laugh now, but it's serious business. You can't fight what you can't see, and you can't see anything! All you can do is keep wiping the sweat out of your eyes and keep guessing where the other guy went. That's genuine stress, in a survival situation!

We see the stress all the time. Watch around the ready room. A guy's getting ready for a tough hop. Personalities come into it. Quiet guys get kinda loud. Loud guys get kinda quiet. They get focused; it's just like athletics. When the hop's over, there's a lot of blowing off steam; they're pumped up for a long time. But all in all, it's a very serious business to these students.

There's a lot of difference between the pilots in training now and those in training when I started out some twenty years ago. Then, you could look outside the hangar and see a row of Corvettes. Today, you see a lot of Volvos, Saabs, pickup trucks. When I was coming up, you'd ask to see a guy's portfolio and you'd get a collection of centerfolds. A portfolio now is all their stocks and mutual funds, those things. The guys now are much smarter, they're more "future oriented" and look at the alternatives more than we did twenty years ago. It's a change of mind-set. We don't find the large numbers of hell-raisers, super-macho, white-scarf pilots in these young students today. They have much longer vision, they have much better plans for the future than we did—but the core is the same. You're gonna find the same things that you found twenty years ago. They're gonna be predominantly first children—first or only children. Statistically, most aviators—those hard-headed enough to pass their way through this—are first children. There are little, curious things like that which make this community of aviators just a little bit different from any other collective group in our society.

We are extremely good at being able to compartmentalize. If I've got a little problem at home—kids having trouble in school or something like that—and I get ready to get into an airplane, that problem at home gets pigeon-holed. We have a much better ability to take all the distractions, corner them, put 'em away, and keep fully focused on the event of the moment—flying the airplane. Mission over, turn the switch in the mind, and then I've got time to take care of the home problems.

STUDENT PILOT

I love flying. My whole time at the Naval Academy I wanted to fly, and frankly, if I couldn't fly I'd leave the Navy as soon as my obligated service was up. Everyone in flight training is "gung-ho" and working hard—it's a real challenge. Going out on the town is tempting, but you just don't feel sharp the next day, so you stay around the base and do your studying thing. Training keeps you humping, but it's fun, just like competitive sports. Everyone is trying to "ace" every step, which is just what I did—up to a point.

RIGHT, IN THE NEWEST TRAINING SYSTEM EMPLOYING STATE-OF-THE-ART TECHNOLOGY, THE T-45 SYSTEM MARRIES SIMULATOR AND CLASSROOM TRAINING WITH A NEW JET TRAINER, THE T-45 GOSHAWK. THE SIMULATOR IS SIMILAR TO THOSE USED BY THE AIRLINE INDUSTRY BUT ALSO PROVIDES A CAPABILITY FOR TRAINING IN FORMATION FLYING, WEAPONS DELIVERY, VARYING LIGHT AND WEATHER CONDITIONS, AND OPERATIONS ASHORE OR ON CARRIERS AT SEA, AND INCLUDES A REALISTIC "FEEL" FOR THE EFFECTS OF MANEUVERS.

My problem is that I was near the top of the class all the way until I came to making a carrier landing. Approaching the "boat," I just freaked out. Something about it made me freeze. They had me come around again—several times—but I just couldn't come down on that little deck. I talked to myself, gave myself hell, and the instructors and LSO [landing signals officer] were helpful, but when it came time to put it down—I just can't explain it! No problem at all in landing jets on land, but no, sir! not on the carrier! Now I'm completing multi-engine training, and I'm doing fine. It's a setback, because I've always been caught up with jets and the Tom Cruise stuff—but I've gotten over the disappointment—I'm still flying! Just a truck instead of a sports car!

THE T-45 GOSHAWK REPLACES BOTH T-2 AND TA-4 JET TRAINERS AS IT MOVES INTO THE TRAINING ESTABLISHMENT. HERE, ON BOARD THE USS *JOHN F. KENNEDY*, A T-45 SMOOTHLY "CATCHES A WIRE," DEMONSTRATING ITS LANDING CAPABILITY. (COURTESY OF MCDONNELL DOUGLAS)

FLIGHT INSTRUCTOR

You're looking at the newest thing, the first of its kind in naval aviation training systems, and I really mean "system." It's a way to train a pilot to fly jets in a minimum of time and at significant savings to the taxpayer. We've stolen a few pages from the exotic simulators used by airlines—this is space age—but the contractor has probably taken it a bit further and better. This is a high-fidelity simulator, which is a principal element of the T-45 Training System, the other elements being the new T-45 Goshawk jet trainer, classroom training with computer-assisted chalkboards featuring video and animation, and contractor logistic support by McDonnell Douglas, who designed and built the whole shebang. This whole thing is just so good, it makes you want to start all over again as a student!

First, the Goshawk is a top-notch trainer with a glass cockpit, digital voice instruments, and a heads-up display. Besides being top of the line, it's a lot more fuel economical and needs a lot less maintenance to keep it in top shape. Everyone who's flown it is just tickled with it. It replaces our two older jet trainers, the T-2 and TA-4, so students have a new era in strike training—training consolidated in one platform, saving lots of flight hours.

But the real fun is this simulator! It represents the product of months of figuring just what a pilot needs to get the feel of flight. It has realistic equipment-reaction times to the hand-eye movements of the pilot, and I think it comes closer to really replicating the actual aircraft reactions than anyone would have thought possible. With this, a pilot can form up with other aircraft and fly formation—or "fly the ball" right onto the flight deck of the boat. See, I've just gone through the "break" and turned to line up with the centerline—I'm just a bit high—now I'm correcting—got it! Students can practice bombing and do all these things while an instructor can kibitz and help them along. Painless! We can give them a wide range of weather effects, so they can get the feel of a pitching and rolling deck, and can give daylight, night, dawn, or dusk. No, I won't go so far as to say that a student pilot can go out and make a perfect carrier landing from just working on the simulator—but they'll come a whole lot closer than before. The bottom line is that it all saves Joe Taxpayer loads of money, if you can believe all the studies that go with getting the system. Time in simulators gets rid of a lot of flight hours with real planes and fuel, so I guess once we've paid for the Buck Rogers stuff, we really save in the long run. From where I sit—or fly—it sure looks good. We sure have come a long way from the "Yellow Peril" [the training model of a bygone day].

HAVING DEMONSTRATED FLIGHT PROFICIENCY IN AN INTERMEDIATE PHASE OF TRAINING, THE NEW AVIATOR ENJOYS A "WINGING" CEREMONY AT WHICH THE COVETED "WINGS OF GOLD" ARE PINNED ON BY HIS WIFE OR GIRLFRIEND, HUSBAND OR BOYFRIEND, PARENT, OR ANOTHER CLOSE OR IMPORTANT PERSON.

THE "BOAT"

The day was overcast and foggy as the plane took off from Naval Air Station, Norfolk, Virginia. The visibility mattered little to its backward-flying passengers, however—only two seats had a window—so most of the dozen or so VIPs were reading or napping despite the roar of the propellers, loud even with the earmuffs in the protective helmets worn by all. The C-2 Greyhound, a "COD"—carrier on-board delivery—carried its passengers and enough mail and freight to make up an eight-thousand-pound load to an aircraft carrier conducting flight operations (flight ops) several hundred miles out in the Atlantic Ocean. As the plane started its descent, tendrils of fog eerily arose from its deck. Two young congressional staffers, not realizing at first that this was only the result of a combination of decreasing cabin pressure, dew point, and the damp atmospheric conditions, watched a bit wide-eyed as the "smoke" rapidly increased to a full-fledged fog inside the cabin. They were only mildly amused at a comment from another that it was "just like going down the old River Styx."

This is the quick and easy way to see and feel carrier operations, appealing to people with busy calendars. Pop out in a COD, feel the jolt of a landing when the plane hooks an arresting wire and jerks to a stop, meet the Captain and receive indoctrination briefings, witness day and night flight operations, tour some of the most important areas of the ship, try to sleep despite the noise and fury of catapults and arresting gear, eat a good dinner and breakfast, and then have the thrill of being catapulted off in a COD to return to terra firma! In all, a compressed and exciting experience that earns admiration for the coordination, stamina, and abilities of five thousand to six thousand young Americans to whom this "buzz saw" or "pressure cooker" life is a daily diet!

OPPOSITE, **A FLIGHT OF F/A-18 HORNETS CIRCLES THE CARRIER USS** *GEORGE WASHINGTON,* **COMING INTO THE LANDING PATTERN, TAILHOOK DOWN FOR AN ARRESTED LANDING. (U.S. NAVY PHOTO, CDR JOHN LEENHOUTS)**

The "boat" is home to scores of aircraft and aviators when at sea. Some say the use of the term "boat" came about because of the very tiny size of the flight deck as seen by a pilot attempting to land on it. Others smile sheepishly when asked why this departure from the proper term "ship," admitting that it probably has more to do with a touch of irreverence on the part of naval aviators who might rebel just a bit at the formality of the "Old Navy." Ship or "boat," it's a marvel of technology and shipbuilding ingenuity.

For starters, it's huge! Picture a building seventeen stories high and as long as three football fields end to end, and almost as wide as one football field is long—in area actually about four and one half acres. Now build into it more than three thousand compartments, offices, or shops. Fill those with the nearly six thousand men and women who make up the crew and air wing, along with all the food, water, and supplies they will require for some months. Then add the reason for the whole thing, the eighty-five to ninety airplanes of seven models, and in all you come up with a powerful ship of about 95,000 tons displacement!

The centerpiece of the ship, of course, is the flight deck. Looking down on it, one sees that an angled "air strip" extends from the stern to about the waist of the ship, where the line of flight extends over the ocean and to the left of the ship's course. When the ship is recovering aircraft, four high-strength wires cross the strip and connect with an arresting-gear-engine assembly. The landing plane is brought to an abrupt stop when its tailhook engages one of the wires. Should the hook fail to engage—a "bolter"—or should the plane be waved off (told to circle around for another landing attempt because the deck is not ready or because the pilot's approach is unsafe), its course is clear of the parked aircraft and of the launches in progress on the two bow catapults that extend from just forward of the "island" (the superstructure that towers over the flight deck) to the bow. Four large hydraulic elevators are installed on the outboard edges of the flight deck in the parking areas, permitting aircraft to be moved between the flight deck and the hangar deck. Smaller bomb elevators connect the flight deck to ammunition magazines deep within the ship, allowing assembled weapons to be brought up for loading on the aircraft.

The heart of operational control for the ship and flight operations is the "island," an eight-story vertical structure on the starboard side of the ship. Halfway up the island is the bridge, from which all of the ship's maneuvering is directed. Here are controlled the rudders that turn the ship; here are given the orders for speed, which must be sent down to the engine rooms; here are found the officer of the deck and the members of the bridge-watch team, who supervise all the efforts needed to drive this enormous structure through the water. Of course, the Captain, the navigator, and the operations officer are very close at

OPPOSITE ABOVE, AN INTERIOR VIEW OF PASSENGERS SEATED FACING AFT IN A C-2 GREYHOUND, THE VEHICLE FOR CARRYING PASSENGERS AND CARGO TO CARRIERS AT SEA, KNOWN AS THE COD, FOR CARRIER ON-BOARD DELIVERY.

OPPOSITE BELOW, A COD AIRCRAFT REVS UP TO FULL POWER. WHEN THE PILOT SIGNALS READINESS WITH A SALUTE TO THE CATAPULT OFFICER (THE "SHOOTER"), THAT OFFICER WILL SIGNAL TO LAUNCH THE COD FROM THE CATAPULT.

FOLLOWING PAGE, A VIEW OF THE NUCLEAR CARRIER USS *GEORGE WASHINGTON,* HERE BEING REPLENISHED BY THE USNS *SANTA BARBARA,* SHOWS THE PERSPECTIVE SEEN BY PILOTS APPROACHING THE "POSTAGE STAMP" OF A FLIGHT DECK IN THE IMMENSITY OF THE OPEN OCEAN. THE NUCLEAR CRUISER USS *BAINBRIDGE* TRAILS IN THE RAINSQUALL AT FAR LEFT.

OPPOSITE, AN OVERHEAD VIEW OF THE GEORGE WASHINGTON ABOUT TO COMMENCE FLIGHT OPERATIONS. EACH TYPE OF AIRCRAFT CARRIED IS VISIBLE AND IDENTIFIABLE, AND THE CHALLENGE OF FITTING IN THE FULL ARRAY OF VARIOUS TYPES CAN BE APPRECIATED. THE TASK CAN BE MET ONLY BECAUSE OF THE FOLDING WINGS AND TAIL SURFACES OF THE AIRCRAFT.

ABOVE, THE USS KITTY HAWK ARRIVES IN SAN DIEGO AND OFF-LOADS CARGO AND THE EQUIPMENT OF THE AIR WING, WHICH HAD "FLOWN TO THE BEACH" THE PREVIOUS DAY. HERE, AIR WING PERSONNEL USE THE HANDY FEATURE OF THE SHIP'S FLIGHT-DECK ELEVATOR TO OFF-LOAD HEAVY GEAR, COMPLETING THE ENTIRE OFF-LOAD IN SEVERAL HOURS.

THE *NIMITZ*-CLASS CARRIER

With the commissioning of the USS *Nimitz* in 1975 a new breed of warship was ushered in—the modern "supercarrier." With the support of a carrier battle group these enormous ships are capable of remaining at sea and carrying out the policy of the United States for months on end, taking naval striking power to wherever it is needed. Home to between 5,000 and 6,000 sailors, it provides a presence that is recognized and respected around the world.

The 100,000 tons of steel and other materials in these magnificent ships form a floating airport that towers more than 20 stories above the waterline and provides a flight deck of 4.5 acres. The embarked air wing is made up of 9 to 10 aircraft squadrons with more than 80 planes. It is nearly 1,100 feet long—just about the length of two Washington Monuments laid end to end—and its two nuclear reactors give it the ability to cover 750 miles per day to shift the area of operations of its aircraft.

Each of these *Nimitz* carriers contains:

- More than 900 miles of cable and wiring
- 60,000 tons of structural steel and about one million pounds of aluminum
- 4 bronze propellers, each measuring 21 feet across and weighing 66,220 pounds
- 2,082 feet of anchor chain, with each of the 684 links weighing 365 pounds, and two anchors weighing 30 tons apiece
- A distillation plant that makes more than 400,000 gallons of fresh water daily, enough to supply 2,000 homes
- Facilities serving 18,150 meals daily
- Nearly 30,000 light fixtures
- 14,000 pillowcases and 28,000 sheets
- 100,000 rolls of toilet paper
- 600,000 ballpoint pens and 1.5 million sheets of paper
- 2,000 telephones

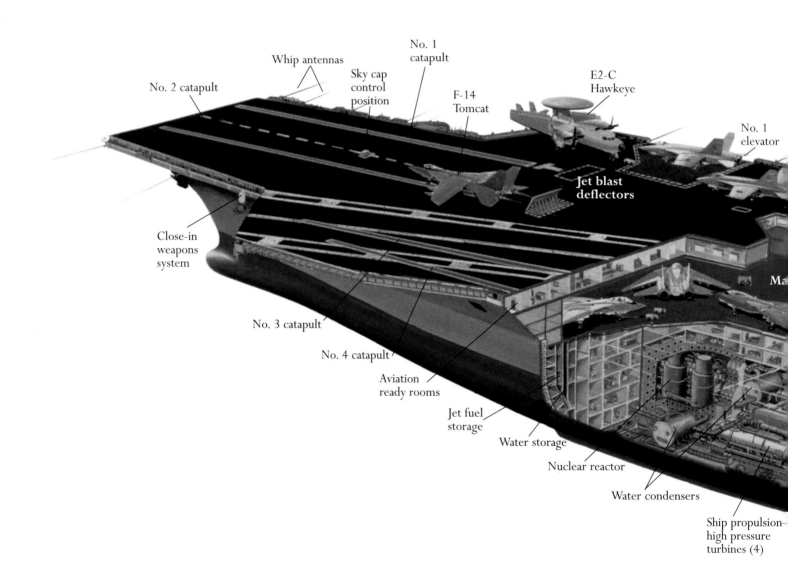

Whip antennas

No. 1 catapult

No. 2 catapult

Sky cap control position

F-14 Tomcat

E2-C Hawkeye

No. 1 elevator

Jet blast deflectors

Close-in weapons system

No. 3 catapult

No. 4 catapult

Aviation ready rooms

Jet fuel storage

Water storage

Nuclear reactor

Water condensers

Ship propulsion– high pressure turbines (4)

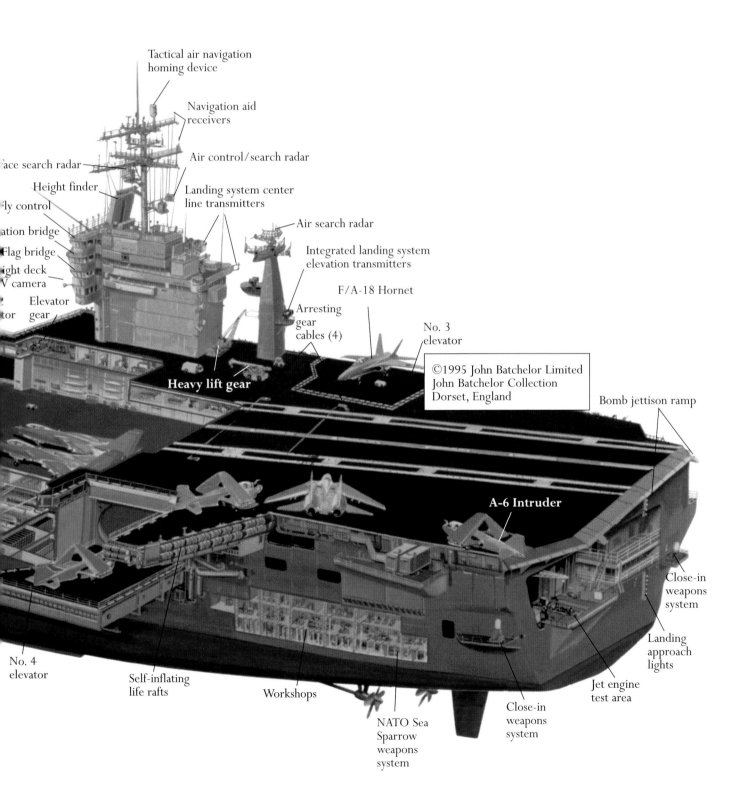

Tactical air navigation
homing device

Navigation aid
receivers

Air control/search radar

...ace search radar

Height finder

Landing system center
line transmitters

...ly control

...ation bridge

...Flag bridge

...ight deck

...V camera

Elevator
...tor   gear

Air search radar

Integrated landing system
elevation transmitters

F/A-18 Hornet

Arresting
gear
cables (4)

No. 3
elevator

Heavy lift gear

©1995 John Batchelor Limited
John Batchelor Collection
Dorset, England

Bomb jettison ramp

A-6 Intruder

Close-in
weapons
system

No. 4
elevator

Self-inflating
life rafts

Workshops

NATO Sea
Sparrow
weapons
system

Close-in
weapons
system

Jet engine
test area

Landing
approach
lights

RIGHT, THE "ISLAND" OF THE *KITTY HAWK*. THIS STRUCTURE HOUSES THE BRIDGE, FLIGHT-DECK CONTROL, PRIMARY FLIGHT CONTROL, FLAG SPACES, AND NAVIGATIONAL SPACES. ELECTRONIC ANTENNAS ARE LOCATED ATOP THE ISLAND TO TAKE ADVANTAGE OF THE HEIGHT ABOVE THE DECK.

BELOW, DEPARTING SAN DIEGO, THE CAPTAIN WATCHES TRAFFIC IN THE CHANNEL CLOSELY AS THE OFFICER OF THE DECK CONNS THE SHIP.

hand or readily available. In fact, though the Captain has an adjacent sea cabin for sleeping and routine administrative work, the Captain's chair on the port side of the bridge is probably the hardest used piece of furniture on board.

The other center of intense activity in the island appears to be a small bridge aft and above the bridge, a tower from which the "air boss" directs flight operations. This is "Pri-Fly," the Primary Flight Operations Center. On the port side of the island, the "air boss" and his assistant, the "mini boss," have an unobstructed view of the flight deck and of the aircraft approaching for landing. In the heat of operations they frequently must make split-second decisions, and the dictatorial atmosphere leaves no doubt as to who is in charge. There's no room for debate or time to study a serious problem. The decision has to be quick—and it has to be right.

Other spaces within the island include the flag bridge, operational areas for the embarked admiral, Air Operations, the navigation center, the signal bridge, the intelligence center, and several staterooms for flag and certain senior officers. In addition, the place of electronics in the busy world of aircraft carriers is obvious from the arrays of radar, radio, and other antennas that bristle from the top of the island structure.

Just below the flight deck and almost at the base of the island lie two important spaces that are brimming with enough space-age electronic equipment and displays to arouse the interest of even the most sophisticated practitioners of the art of the byte and megabyte. The Combat Direction Center (CDC) is the "nerve center" of the ship, the place where air-, submarine-, and surface-contact data, as well as any noteworthy geographical features, are automatically fused into a coherent, though complex, picture. Status boards alert decision makers to vital tactical information. Defensive-weapons directors are located to permit their rapid use by the tactical action officers, the supervisors of this electronic wonderland, should the situation demand. Close by CDC is the somewhat similar appearing Carrier Air Traffic Control Center (CATCC), from which the ship's aircraft are controlled in a manner analogous to the control of airplanes at a busy commercial airport.

For a visitor, just finding the assigned sleeping compartment or mess hall is a challenge, and getting about the ship is great exercise. Moving from deck to deck, one encounters steep ladders with occasional noggin-knocking low clearances guaranteed to compress several vertebrae. Trips from the flight deck to the bridge leave sedentary souls perspiring and puffing. Having been toured about the ship for a while, one becomes aware that there are ship-length passageways port and starboard below the hangar deck, truly superhighways for moving fore and aft rapidly. Otherwise, to move along any other passageway, one has to be a college hurdler. Frames, or structural supports, essen-

THIS FORE-AND-AFT PASSAGEWAY EXTENDS VIRTUALLY THE LENGTH OF THE SHIP. FRAME STRUCTURES PROVIDE A HURDLES-LIKE OBSTACLE COURSE, REPLETE WITH WHAT THE CREW REFERS TO AS "KNEE-KNOCKERS."

tial to the ship's construction intersect at regular intervals—and at knee height—but the athlete gets the beat: seven strides between hurdles . . . stride-stride-stride-hurdle . . . stride-stride-stride-hurdle! Ask in the wardroom how to get to the nearest head (toilet), and the answer comes not in terms of the compartment's designation—a slurry of letters and numbers that only the engineers use—but aviator-simplified "Go out the door, turn left, go just past the third knee-knocker, and turn right!" Simple!

The body's senses are maxed out as soon as one steps aboard, particularly if flight operations are under way. Noise, and *what noise*! Blasting heat! Smells—oil, jet fuel, jet exhaust! Colors—lights—the flashing flame of engines in afterburner! Only the sense of taste seems not to play, but not for long—even that is sated by the array of foods and beverages available below-decks. If, in our Navy, a submarine is a tomb, a carrier is a roaring volcano. Even with ears protected by special helmets with ear muffs—"cranials"—one is overpowered by the roar of the jets, and anywhere—*anywhere*—that one is not inside closed doors on or above the flight deck, one's hearing is in danger of permanent damage without that protection. In some especially loud areas, one notes a warning sign that *double* protection is required—the muffs, plus foam plugs placed inside the ear passages. Communication on the flight deck is by hand signal for the majority of workers or by words shouted against one's ear covering. Lanes painted on the flight deck indicate "foul" territory—those areas that are life threatening during launches and landings to anyone not inside an aircraft. As aircraft launches are alternated between two adjacent catapults, an observer finds himself being helpfully tugged back to safety behind the proper line, and he learns to crouch to minimize the blast effect of the departing plane's jets, thus remaining on board the ship! A visitor feels the pulsating power and vibration as the engines are brought to full power and mutters, "Good God!" as the plane catapults off just beyond touching distance. An awesome experience!

While flight operations by day are an experience, night operations present an extravaganza! Old pilots shake their heads and give off wry smiles when asked about night carrier landings. Some may not admit to fear, but all will testify to a marked increase in the "pucker factor," usually experienced as a tightening of the sphincter. A former F-14 squadron commander discussed the eeriness and hostility of landing in almost total blackness, when depth perception is a near impossibility: "Throw in a pitching deck and a thunderstorm; it's like practicing bleeding." Most experienced pilots can relate gripping accounts of shipmates who approached disaster, who repeatedly bolted, who had to hook up again and again with the airborne tanker just to have enough gas to make another stab at the deck, and who kept getting "waved off" for being too low before finally catching a wire. There are

opportunities aplenty for a "wrenching experience" for a carrier pilot, and for forty to fifty sailors—officer and bluejacket—who race in darkness or blazing sun on decks made slippery from rain, sleet, or oil spills, and who crouch below life-threatening jet intakes or propellers to chock or unchock, chain or unchain, or attach aircraft to catapult mechanisms. Watching such an operation in minus-thirty windchill, one concludes that there's not much that's harder!

The Captain could sell tickets to his crew to watch flight operations at any time, but especially at night. From the anticipation and high interest displayed by sailors from all departments of the ship, it is obvious that there is a strong "team" feeling and pride in conducting flight operations professionally. As the hour grows near for their start, "Vultures' Row" is packed. This long platform high up on the island is buffeted by the winds coming across the deck and provides little protection from the weather, but it gives a clear view fore and aft. Crew

THE SETTING SUN SILHOUETTES SAILORS ON THE SIGNAL BRIDGE, SAN DIEGO AND THE CORONADO BRIDGE FADING INTO THE DISTANCE AS THE *KITTY HAWK* HEADS OUT TO SEA.

members wait for a turn at the rail for the entertainment of observing good traps and bad, and to feel the heat blast of jet exhaust and the thunder and vibration of engines as they roar to full power. Even the added distance from another vantage point—the signal bridge on top of the island—does little to lessen any of these effects. To the photographer intent upon capturing stirring photos from this exposed spot, the vibration and winds as well as the heat-wave distortion are tough enough opponents, but he is soon discouraged by yet another presence. The cyclic sweep of powerful radars becomes an enemy, setting up electronic interference that flashes strobes not even turned on and takes control of fully automatic cameras and motor drives, exposing rolls of film and damaging expensive printed components in the doing—even though nary a button was pressed! But the view is superb.

On the flight deck, reflective tape on helmets and flotation jackets

JET ENGINES ROAR AND AFTERBURNERS ERUPT FLAME AS AN F-14 TOMCAT LAUNCHES FROM THE *KITTY HAWK*'S CATAPULT AT NIGHT. S-3 VIKINGS AND A-6 INTRUDERS ARE ILLUMINATED.

picks up the low-level lighting from the island. The effect is that of a large swarm of fireflies busily moving about the deck in the parking and catapult areas forward, and in the landing area aft. There are blinking red lights, blue lights, and green lights about the deck, but the great swarms are the yellow lights reflected from the aircraft handlers. Chemically activated wands are waved, giving directions to aircraft moving from parking areas to approach areas to the catapults, and lights on the tractors weave glowworm patterns. A protective circle of "fireflies" forms about a moving aircraft, and arm movements cause circles or erratic zigzags of light to trace against the darkness. In the landing area, final checks of the arresting assemblies are made, and LSOs move to their platform. The ship will recover aircraft that were catapulted off two hours before and will launch another complete flight.

From the enclosed comfort of the bridge, conversations and orders can be heard distinctly—quite unlike "Vultures' Row." Just minutes before flight ops begin, the officer of the deck (OOD) gives rudder and course orders to the helmsman and turns the ship into the wind, producing maximum wind across the deck to aid in landing and launching aircraft. As the ship settles on the launch course, both the Captain and OOD closely observe the indicators that show wind across the deck and crosswind. Small course changes are ordered to reduce crosswind to a permissible level, and the Captain explains that the wind is adequate to permit the ship to advance at only a moderate speed during flight ops. An SH-3 Sikorsky Sea King helicopter has been launched to serve as a plane guard, its crew ready to leap out from the hovering craft to retrieve any pilot or aircrewman who should have the misfortune—very rare—of a water landing.

First off this night are the Grumman E-2C Hawkeyes. Propeller-driven and slower than other planes, they need more time to get on station, but up and ready they must be, for they are the advance sensors and controllers for the fighters and other aircraft, as well as serving as the admiral's big "eye in the sky." Next off the deck are the fighters—McDonnell Douglas F/A-18 Hornets and Grumman F-14 Tomcats. As the first roars to full power prior to launching, its afterburners light up the catapult area, and the plane traces a colorful path into the darkness. Dazzling! But the real thriller this night is the takeoff of the F-14, a model with an earlier-design engine, which in afterburner produces a screaming inferno lighting up the flight deck and the ocean, resembling more a rocket launching from Cape Kennedy than a piloted aircraft being catapulted from a carrier deck!

The flight deck is a kaleidoscope of lights as the crew scuttles about, giving hand signals, moving aircraft to the catapult, hooking them up, raising the jet-blast deflectors that direct jet exhaust upward, and getting planes in the air.

With the start of night landings, there seems to be a bit more "focus" than during daylight operations. Not tension; tension seems not to be a tangible factor anywhere. There just seems to be a bit closer attention to the status of the deck, more questions regarding the fuel levels of individual aircraft, more exchanges between the air boss and the Captain, a closer watch on the crosswind—a hardly noticeable tightening of procedures, subconsciously reflecting the more difficult conditions and perhaps the memories of past night landings. In Pri-Fly it is all business. With the aid of binoculars, each aircraft in the landing pattern is identified in turn by the configuration of its lights. The aircraft type is checked against the weights and wire settings. The Air Operations Center is queried regarding any training requirements, and representatives from the air wing and the squadrons are there to provide information to the pilots in case of mechanical trouble. Aircraft land with the thud of thirty-some tons traveling at 150 knots, catch a wire as they roar to full power, then with a "foul deck" signal showing, are hastily moved to a parking area—just in time to give a "clear deck" signal to the oncoming aircraft.

Night operations completed, a tired Captain consults with the navigator and writes and signs the "night order book," which details any desires regarding night movements, instructions regarding ship traffic, and reports to be received regarding just how much distance the carrier should maintain from other shipping, and sets forth the particulars for a rendezvous with a replenishment tanker at daybreak. The Captain will rest well, knowing that a well-trained and alert bridge watch will keep the ship safe, an equally competent engineering watch will ensure that the ship will get where its supposed to and have water and electricity, and that bread will be baked, laundry washed, and the injured and sick attended to in this city at sea.

CAPTAIN

This assignment is something I've worked all of my adult life for, and something I've wanted so long and so hard I could taste it! Command of a carrier! You know, you work all the stops up to this point—flight training, wings, division officer, squadron executive officer [XO] and commanding officer [CO], flying off carriers with air wings—that's the flying part. Then you get selected for higher-responsibility jobs. Some are carrier XOs, navigators, staff jobs—almost all get a tour in Washington, just to see if they can stand torture, you know. But then you get a "deep draft" command—a large ship that gives us aviators a firsthand crash course in driving big ships. It's a real challenge, plus being a hell of a lot of fun! Then, if you make the "cut," you get to command one of these beautiful things! We probably ought to have to pay for the privilege!

ABOVE, **THE CAPTAIN OF THE USS** *KITTY HAWK* **FINDS TIME FOR ADMINISTRATIVE WORK BETWEEN FLIGHT OPS IN HIS SEA CABIN ADJACENT TO THE BRIDGE.**

ABOVE, THE CAPTAIN OF THE USS *GEORGE WASHINGTON* SPENDS HOURS EACH DAY OBSERV-ING THE CONDUCT OF FLIGHT OPERATIONS FROM HIS CHAIR ON THE BRIDGE.

RIGHT, FAR LESS AUSTERE THAN A SEA CABIN, THE CAPTAIN'S IN-PORT CABIN AND MESS ARE FACILITIES THAT CAN BE MADE UP TO ENTERTAIN DIGNITARIES IN STYLE, AND FIND MUCH USE AS THE *KITTY HAWK* DEPLOYS AND SHOWS THE FLAG IN OTHER COUN-TRIES.

Some folks ask how it feels to have such an "awesome" responsibility—well, it really doesn't feel all that awesome. The way one comes up in the Navy, you're always cutting your teeth on increasing responsibility, so it seems just a very natural progression, step by step, right up to becoming the Chief of Naval Operations—I have to guess at that last point! And you know, all of us *like* responsibility—we *thrive* on it! That's why we're in the Navy.

You know, you're right to call this ship a "city at sea." We've got everything a small city has, right down to a jail—and one heck of an airport! I run the city—some say like a mayor (others say dictator)—with a fantastic amount of help. One visitor likened my job to the manager of a huge industrial facility and complex—not a bad observation, what with the variety and scope of facilities we have. Personally, though, I think we overplay the "manage" thing a bit these days, especially when we speak of "battle management"—the Navy doesn't *manage* battles, it *fights* them—with good people, with *leadership,* and with good aggressive training that leads to proper decisions when all the unexpected things happen. Those things aren't managed.

The XO is my right-hand man, second in command, and we both are helped in virtually everything we do by the command master chief—at times there's little doubt in our minds that we *really* work for *him!* Leadership is the name of the game with these two people, and they probably wear out a pair of shoes a week, walking to every corner of the ship and checking on things and seeing people. They coordinate and schedule all ship activities through the officer department heads and through the leading chief petty officers and petty officers. Leadership is what makes it go at every level, not just the top, and you'll see it right down to the nonrated young sailors—watch our plane captains, for example, and those "yellow shirt" directors on the flight deck!

I think that all of our carriers are super. Each CO knows he's got the best ship, naturally. The thing that I really feel good about in this one is the way five thousand to six thousand young people—and I *mean* young: average age about twenty—work together with spirit and enthusiasm despite being absolutely overworked and under-rested for months on end. Our communications have to be classed as outstanding. We keep all hands "cut in" on each and every event—tell them when they're good or bad—and we go on closed-circuit TV to explain policies and changes in plans. We try to keep from having surprises! The modern Navy does a great job of taking care of people, and we spend a lot of time at every level to get rid of minor irritations or unnecessary regulations. These young guys are very bright, and they really like doing what they do. They're proud, and they damned well should be! And I'm proud of *them!*

ABOVE, "PRI-FLY" IS THE DOMAIN OF THE AIR BOSS, WHO MAINTAINS CONTROL OF THE FLIGHT DECK FROM A VANTAGE POINT AT THE TOP OF THE TOWER. BELOW, CREWMEN OPERATE TV CAMERAS TO RECORD EVERY LANDING, WHICH CAN BE VIEWED THROUGHOUT THE SHIP ON CLOSED-CIRCUIT CHANNELS. HERE AN F/A-18 HORNET IS ABOUT TO "CATCH A WIRE" AND LAND ON THE FLIGHT DECK OF THE *KITTY HAWK.*

The "air boss" is head of the Air Department of the ship, but basically when at sea it's a total effort controlling the launch and recovery of airplanes and all that goes with that—I kinda "own" the airplanes as long as they're within five miles of the ship. Once they take off and are beyond that range, they go about the business assigned by the CAG [commander, carrier air wing]—practicing intercepts, bombing exercises, sometimes just "RDA" [random dance around], whatever.

Everything on the hangar deck or flight deck—moving planes, positioning or "spotting" them, fueling and fixing them, checking that the catapults and arresting gear are in top shape—we do all of that with the help of about eight hundred people. My assistant, the "mini boss," and I will be up here in the Primary Flight tower whenever we have flight ops—two hours, six hours, twenty-four hours, you name it—and those young guys you see down there in all of those colored shirts will keep us company. The old salts used to say, "You already know how to sleep, now learn how to stay awake for a while." We have! The only person who gets less sleep is the Captain. We usually have several other people up here too. During certain evolutions (Navy parlance for an event, scheduled or accidental) there may be reps from the squadrons. That man is writing backwards on that clear plastic status board so that we can read the data. The man with binoculars is very important—he calls the type of the incoming plane to double-check against the tension set on the arresting gear—too much for the weight of the plane would cause a tremendous jerk, perhaps damage, and too little would let it go too far down the deck. At night he reads the type of aircraft by the configuration of its lights.

Ours is a constant job of not only controlling all aircraft movements, but we are totally caught up in assuring the safety of personnel—keeping people in the proper clothing, training them in the rapid repair of vital equipment, keeping their heads out of engine intakes,

BELOW, **THE AIR BOSS'S TOWER PROVIDES A FULL AND UNOBSTRUCTED VIEW OF THE FLIGHT DECK, WITH THE COMMUNICATION FACILITIES NECESSARY TO CONTROL THE MOVEMENT OF AIRCRAFT AS WELL AS COORDINATE WITH THE CAPTAIN AND THE BRIDGE WATCH WHO ARE CONTROLLING THE SHIP.**

protecting aircraft, etc. We keep in radio contact with aircraft and by phone with "paddles," the LSO back over there across the flight deck, and also with the bridge, Air Operations, and Flight-Deck Control. You just heard the Captain asking about giving that last Hornet another landing for practice. I also use this 5-MC [flight-deck announcing system] to really "focus" the action when I need to, and I have a flight-deck radio system to work with the flight deck. You just heard me being nasty and announcing, "Have that sailor who dropped his key ring from 'Vulture's Row' report to me in Pri-Fly as soon as he's picked it up!" That could have resulted in FOD [foreign object damage] to an engine—a plane lost or even a life. I'll eat the kid out pretty hard but then slap him on the back when I'm finished: he did what he's been trained to do—reported it right away—so we held up flight ops for a few minutes until we found the keys. He'll feel a little stupid for a while, but I'll bet he's a hell of a lot more careful with his keys in the future!

AIRCRAFT HANDLING OFFICER—"THE HANDLER"

I'm the air boss's man in the barrel down here on the flight deck. I control all movement of aircraft on the flight deck and hangar deck from Flight-Deck Control. I've got some outstanding and fantastically experienced people who are what you might say "in automatic" when we conduct flight ops. They know their jobs and march off on what's

BELOW, A GIANT MOBILE CRANE IS PART OF THE FLIGHT DECK'S SPECIALIZED EQUIPMENT, FACILITATING THE MOVING AND HOISTING OF AIRCRAFT. THE CRANE ON THE *KITTY HAWK* IS HEAVY ENOUGH THAT A SPECIAL POSITION IS PRESCRIBED TO AVOID UNFAVORABLE SHIP'S TRIM WHEN TRAVERSING SHALLOW SPOTS IN SAN DIEGO CHANNEL.

needed; it's not like this is the first time around. Right in front of me I have the entire flight deck layout, to scale, and the little models of aircraft are to scale. We can fit them into spots here before we really have to move them out there. On that shelf below we have the same thing for the hangar deck. Those little colored pins? We stick them into the aircraft models to show us that there's something we have to do about them—repairs, fuel, weapons, whatever. Our people here maintain a running maintenance status of every aircraft on board—its weapon systems, etc.—and we coordinate with the weapons, intermediate maintenance, supply, air ops, and strike ops officers. I also coordinate all space allocation on the flight deck and hangar deck between other departments—as well as the use of elevators. Even though it all seems huge, there's really limited space.

That flail you saw just a few minutes ago—not routine, but never totally unexpected—that's an example of how good planning goes out the window when stuff hits the fan, but it also shows how our sailors can react when they're trained like ours are. We were getting ready to fly the air wing off to the beach and had the aircraft made up in several flights back on the aft part of the deck. You know, planes of similar types, flights that would fly in formation—all neat and organized. Well, that COD flight with passengers heading for the beach—includ-

ABOVE, **THE AIRCRAFT-HANDLING OFFICER MOVES AIRCRAFT ON THE FLIGHT AND HANGAR DECKS AS ON A GIANT CHESS-BOARD, KEEPING TRACK OF POSITION AND STATUS WITH SCALE-MODEL PLANES.**

FOLLOWING PAGE, **THE** *SARATOGA'S* **FLIGHT DECK, LESS SPACIOUS THAN THAT OF** *NIMITZ-*CLASS CARRIERS, PRESENTS THE AIR BOSS AND FLIGHT-DECK CREW WITH DIFFICULT PROBLEMS, AS SEEN HERE WITH A SWARM OF F/A-18, S-3, AND A-6 AIRCRAFT. A LINE OF CREW MEMBERS CONDUCTS A METHODI-CAL FOD WALKDOWN, LOOKING FOR AND PICKING UP ANY ITEM THAT COULD PRODUCE FOD—FOREIGN OBJECT DAMAGE—IF INGESTED INTO A JET ENGINE.**

ing the Army general—had a problem shortly after takeoff. The pilot reported he had an electrical fire on board, was trying to put it out, and would head back to the boat! But he sure as hell couldn't land with all those planes stacked up back there! Well, as you saw, we had people running all about, moving airplanes, and we started shooting them off—first on the cat [catapult], first off—with hardly more than enough interval to build up cat pressure. We may have set some sort of record for cat shots—it was very, very exciting. But we got the deck cleared and the wires set just about the time he announced the fire was out—we'd have been able to land him and put out the fire. Our nice plan was shot, but it was a great drill! I hope the various flights find each other on their way home so they can do their things!

HANGAR DECK LEADING PETTY OFFICER

I work here in Hangar-Deck Control, and my immediate boss is the hangar deck chief and above him the hangar deck officer. We're responsible for planning and supervising all aircraft movement, handling, and security down here as well as maintaining the hangar deck. We operate damage-control and fire-fighting equipment also. We have "conflagration stations" at several viewpoints above the hangar, with people on watch there all the time. I guess you might think that "conflagration" is a fancy way to say "fire," but if we were to get a serious fire down here, with aircraft parked and it jammed full, it would not be just a fire, it'd be one hell of a fire! So in carriers we have a special category to name one hell of a fire. I have to see that when we park aircraft here we can always shut those heavy steel doors that can divide the hangar deck in case of fire. The job is really a challenge, fitting the different types of planes in, and moving them without banging them together. Look at the deck now—really crowded. People always ask how we can play basketball games here—they've seen that in movies or photos. Answer is, we don't, most of the time when the air wing is aboard. Of course, we always have a few jocks who just have to get their jogging in down here, even when they have to duck wing and tail edges, and all of those airplane hold-down holes every few feet don't make ankles any stronger. It helps give the "docs" practice, though, stitching and splinting.

AIRCRAFT CRASH AND SALVAGE OFFICER—"THE AIR BOATSWAIN"

Yeah, I just go by the name "Boats," not that long title. I have a number of flight-deck personnel assigned to our "crash" crew for the very specialized jobs of fighting fires on the flight deck, pulling people out from crashed aircraft in minimum time, and clearing flight-deck crash-

THE VERY CROWDED HANGAR DECK OF THE USS *GEORGE WASHINGTON*.

es. We're up here and ready to handle aircraft emergencies during flight quarters and general quarters. You remember some of those World War II documentaries, showing shot-up planes crash-landing on the deck and the crew pushing the wrecks or burning planes into the drink? That's us—but fortunately, we haven't had a war recently where we had to handle that sort of thing, at least not that way.

I train the people, and I'm responsible for maintaining the equipment we use. Those young sailors wearing the silver fire-fighting suits put in very long days, and those suits aren't designed for cool comfort. Imagine putting twelve to sixteen hours in those things in the Persian Gulf or off Haiti! They earn their pay.

I'll give you an example of how fast these crash crews work and how it pays off. Not long ago one of our carriers in the Pacific had an F-14 hit the ramp on landing—a tremendous crash. Both the pilot and RIO [radar intercept officer] ejected in a split second as it hit—it almost seemed they wouldn't have time, but they did. The crash guys were on the plane in seconds. The RIO came down in the water and was picked up OK, but the worst possible thing for the pilot—he came down on the flight deck right in the center of the fireball! Training and guts paid off—the crash crew had him out in seconds and the fire out in about thirty seconds. Badly burned, but alive and hospitalized, and he's expected to totally recover and be back to flying! Five guys in the crash crew were given medals—a hard way to get one!

LEFT, **THE CRASH CREW ON THE** *SARATOGA* **IS CONSTANTLY READY DURING FLIGHT OPERATIONS, ENCASED IN HEAT-REFLECTING SUITS AND WITH MOBILE EQUIPMENT AT THE READY TO RESPOND IN SPLIT SECONDS TO FIGHT A FIRE OR PULL A SHIPMATE OUT OF A FIREBALL.**

"BLUE SHIRTS"—AIRCRAFT HANDLING CREW

When you see a plane or helo come in for a landing, you'll see us in action. If it's a helo, you'll see a "yellow shirt" directing him to his spot, then you'll see one or two of us—"blue shirts"—rushing out to put

chocks under his wheels to keep him in position on the deck before anyone can leave the helo. If it's an airplane, the LSO directs his arrested landing, then a "yellow shirt" signals him—or now it may be a her—where to taxi to the "spot" [the plane's assigned parking spot]. At that point, we chock the wheels and chain the airplane to those padeyes you see all over the flight deck and hangar deck. Once we chain the plane, it's secure. Don't worry about those heavy rolls from the sea or the list from using rudder on the ship—once we chain it, it'll stay!

The tractors you see moving about the deck are driven by "blue shirts"; so are the starting units for starting up the airplanes. In fact, we operate all the handling equipment. Other "blue shirts" whom we call the "EOs"—elevator operators—operate those large aircraft elevators that move planes between the flight deck and the hangar deck. You can tell them by their white helmets.

When we have planes revving up, you may see "blue shirts" along with all the other colors of shirts surrounding a moving aircraft in a big

ABOVE, "BLUE SHIRTS" STAND READY TO CHOCK AND LOCK IN POSITION AN EA-6B PROWLER AIRCRAFT JUST AFTER LANDING.

circle to keep people from wandering in and getting hurt—if a prop is turning, the whole circle is rotating their hands to make the evolution obvious to someone who might enter it. Safety is the rule for all of us. If we see you with your goggles not in place, any one of us will tell you about it, whether you're an admiral or head cleaner. Same goes for flotation jackets not buttoned, or carrying loose objects which could "FOD" a jet engine. Our work is tough and dangerous enough—we don't need carelessness.

"BROWN SHIRTS"—PLANE CAPTAINS

I'm a plane captain. The F-14 behind me has my name on it, and my hometown. It doesn't belong to me—the pilot owns it some, too. His name's on it, too; so's the RIO's. Yeah, I'm kinda proud of my job, and I like it. I like my pilot and RIO too. They're probably the best in the squadron. That probably sounds like kid stuff—but I believe it. You feel pretty important, knowing that they trust you with seeing that the plane is ready to fly.

We're air wing personnel; we're not "ship's company." We stay with the airplane, except for flying in it. When the plane is on the beach and the air wing is not deployed or doing exercises with the boat, we're on the beach, watching out for and checking out the plane. When the boat is going to deploy, the plane captains and other squadron personnel come aboard with all of the wing's equipment while the boat's still in port. Then the air wing flies aboard when the boat gets out to where it has sea room to head into the wind for recovery of aircraft.

We do a complete checkout before the pilot gets to the plane—a lot of mandatory steps, looking for things that might be troublesome. We check it often and, I guess, always. For some things, we call in the "green shirts" to do maintenance. You might think of us as a filling-station guy—checking things out but if it's too complex calling in a mechanic—except we don't fill the gas tank, the "grapes" do that. You see us unchaining the planes a lot, and carrying chains away. One of our plane captains is so little that a big load of chains sometimes drags him right down to the deck!

Most of us are nonrated, meaning we haven't been in the Navy long enough to be a third-class petty officer. A couple of our plane captains are third class. We feel pretty damned important to have a big load so soon, and to be so trusted. I was a dropout before I enlisted, but this duty has made me grow up a lot. I like my job, and if I stick with the Navy, I only want duty in carriers. They're the best, and you don't get seasick. You know you're on the front line of whatever the country's trying to do. But right now, I've just about decided to leave after this hitch and go to college. Hey, who knows? Maybe after that I'll come back and fly one of these babies!

OPPOSITE, A MOBILE-EQUIPMENT OPERATOR, A "BLUE SHIRT," DRIVES A VEHICLE SWEEPING UP FOREIGN OBJECTS FROM THE FLIGHT DECK.

ON THE *SARATOGA*, A PLANE CAPTAIN
MAKES FINAL ADJUSTMENTS TO THE AIR-
CRAFT'S SYSTEMS PRIOR TO FLIGHT.

THE *KITTY HAWK* PLANE CAPTAINS JOKE
ABOUT THE WEIGHT OF THE HEAVY STEEL
CHAINS THAT THEY HAVE JUST UNHOOKED
FROM THEIR AIRCRAFT PREPARATORY TO
FLIGHT OPERATIONS.

OPPOSITE, A PLANE CAPTAIN, A "BROWN
SHIRT," READIES HIS F/A-18 HORNET FOR
MORNING FLIGHT OPERATIONS.

MARINE PILOT

One of these guys really saved me one day! I had just landed on the carrier, and the director had moved me over to the parking area, near the edge of the deck. The "pushers" were pushing me into a parking position as close to the deck edge as possible, when the ship changed course to port—fairly fast—so that the deck listed on the down side. At this point the pushers weren't pushing—they didn't have to! I was now rolling slowly on an overboard course! At this point an extremely alert and experienced chief leaped out, grabbed a set of chains, and hooked the hook of one end into one of the hold-down fittings in the flight deck. He raced to my nosewheel and wrapped the chain several turns around it and held on. We rolled back a bit more, then came to a sudden, jerking halt. The nose leaped way up, then crashed down toward the deck, and the chief held on! That simple rapid action saved my bacon and my aircraft—and it goes on all the time!

CATAPULT OFFICER—THE "SHOOTER"

The flight deck officer is the one over there amidships in the yellow shirt, with "DECK" on his back. It's his job to plan and direct all air-craft handling on the flight deck, including parking and security, and to set the sequences for launching to minimize the time required to build up steam pressure for the next launch. That sometimes gives him a "jig-saw puzzle" type of thing since the different types of aircraft vary in weight considerably—which calls for different steam pressures. If there's a large jump in weights, there may be delays and wasted time. We like a smooth, "Bam! Bam! Bam!" type of launch sequence. Add to this that he has to have a good feel for which plane has to be on station first, who has the farthest to go, and he has to have a computer in his head. Tough job! The flight deck chief "calls the deck"—meaning that he makes split-second decisions when sorting and prioritizing aircraft on their way to the catapults and positioning them after landing. He's kinda the central figure on the flight deck.

Once the aircraft is moved into position on the catapult, we raise the JBD [jet-blast deflector], a high steel door that deflects the blast from the plane upward. Here I take over the operation. As the catapult officer, or "shooter," I'm responsible for the whole catapult crew, the aircraft weight verification, and the catapult launch settings. I signal the pilot to rev up to full power, get the signals from our crew that each step is complete, check the panels again, and make sure that the plane's in the proper configuration and the pilot's head is back against the seat. If he's all set, the pilot salutes me—at night he turns on his lights—I salute the pilot, take another look to see that the deck is clear, and take my stooping position and touch the deck. Then, all set, I point two fin-gers toward the bow, and the catapult operator fires the catapult. The

air boss can break this sequence and stop the launch with a button he has up in Pri-Fly if he sees something wrong. But otherwise, the plane's on its way, building up to 150 knots in about two seconds!

On *Nimitz*-class carriers the "shooter" sits in a "bubble" near the catapults and has an enlisted observer with him. He's out of the weather and blast, and I guess he misses some of the romance of feeling the heat and blast that almost knock you over—but I'd probably vote for it on wet days or when the windchill is minus thirty!

IN *NIMITZ*-CLASS CARRIERS, THE CATAPULT OFFICER—THE "SHOOTER"—PERFORMS IN THE RELATIVE LUXURY OF A "BUBBLE" WHILE CHECKING THE FINAL STEPS IN PREPARATION TO LAUNCH THE NEXT AIR-CRAFT.

"YELLOW SHIRTS"—FLIGHT DECK DIRECTORS

Our main job is directing the movement of planes on the flight deck—the "roof," as we call it. We tell the pilots where to move their birds and give them hand signals to guide them between obstacles to their "spot" for takeoff or tie-down. No—absolutely no—aircraft moves on the roof unless it's under the control of a "yellow shirt"—a director. The same goes for tractors. We're like traffic cops up here. We're pretty young—as a group they say we average about twenty-four years old, but that includes some of the real old guys like that first class over there—thirty-seven years old, and he's been doing this for eighteen years! It took me over two years to qualify, and I'm still learning.

It's a very dangerous place, the flight deck during air operations. There's roaring noise all around you, you wear "cranials"—head-protecting helmets and earmuffs—and flotation jackets—life jackets equipped with dyes, whistles, and lights—it's easy to whack your head, and if you don't watch out, you can get blown over the side by the jet blast.

We're a real team, watching out for each other. When a jet engine revs up, you can get sucked up into the intake. We're all taught to curl up into a ball if that happens, but you'd better pray too. A prop whirling can do a lot worse than make a new part in your hair. Keep looking around; on the flight deck you need eyes in the back of your noggin. See that JBD there? One time we had a Hawkeye revving up, and its prop wash bounced around the JBD, unexpectedly hitting a guy on his side—like a clip in football. His feet were dangling in the air, and he was hanging onto another plane for dear life to keep from going overboard when we got to him.

Most of us had to work our way up. We started out as "blue shirts," the guys who chock up the airplanes and chain them down, and qualified as tractor drivers. There's a very formal step-by-step training and qualification program, and it takes some months or years to get it all done. We've got an important job—all weather, any place, any time! We cut it!

"GREEN SHIRTS"—CATAPULT CREW HOLD-BACK MAN

We make up two crews on the flight deck, the catapult crew and the arresting-gear crew. Watch flight ops, you'll see us all over the deck. We're the working guys—the "yellow shirts" direct, we do. My job is to attach the hold-back unit to the aircraft to hold it in place prior to launch. That's a metal link that has a thinner-diameter neck, which can take just so much tension, then breaks at the proper time, letting the plane free to go down the catapult with the shuttle. Other "cat" crew people are the topside petty officer, who monitors and supervises the hookup procedure before each launch, and the center-deck operator—he communicates with Catapult Control, relaying aircraft type, gross weight, and side number. The catapult setting is figured using wind across the deck and airplane weight as inputs into the graph, then picking off the setting to produce the desired aircraft speed—we give them about ten knots more than the minimum needed. The weight-board operator verifies the aircraft gross weight with the aircraft crew as a final check before launch—there's a lot of difference in weights of the different types of planes.

Our JBD operator raises and lowers the deflectors for each aircraft. You'll see him get the signal just after the aircraft moves onto the catapult and pulls forward clear of the JBD. He'll lower it to let the aircraft move onto the cat. The JBD prevents jet blast from injuring per-

A "GREEN SHIRT" SHOWS THE WEIGHT BOARD TO THE PILOT AND TO THE CATAPULT OFFICER. THIS ASSURES THAT THE WEIGHT OF THE AIRCRAFT IN ITS PARTICULAR CONFIGURATION AND LOADING IS PROPERLY SET ON THE CATAPULT EQUIPMENT.

sonnel and aircraft aft of the launch area, but even with it you'll feel plenty of jet blast as you and aircraft move about the deck. Another "green shirt," the deck-edge operator, over on the side of each catapult on the catwalk, actually "fires" the catapult on the command of the catapult officer—the "shooter." Up forward, the bow safety man makes sure the forward part of the ship is clear of personnel and foreign objects before and during launches. We don't have many slack times—we sleep soundly when we get the chance!

"GREEN SHIRTS"—ARRESTING-GEAR CREW

As the topside petty officer of the arresting-gear crew, I work for the gear officer, whom you will see across the deck from the LSO. He's responsible for making sure—making dead certain—that the proper weight is set in the arresting-gear engines for each type of aircraft. Each has a max trap weight, and you may see an E-2C, for example, dumping gas while still in the pattern before trapping. I monitor and supervise the equipment and gear personnel prior to the recovery of aircraft. Obviously, the most important thing before flight ops is to visually check the four wires entirely. During recovery ops, "green shirts" work as deck-edge operators, stationed in the catwalk, and retract the wires after the recovery of aircraft. Hook runners keep the

VIEWED FROM THE CATWALK OF THE SARATOGA, AN F/A-18 HORNET IS CAUGHT BY THE CAMERA AT THE MOMENT OF LEAVING THE CATAPULT.

FOLLOWING PAGE, WHEN TIME IS OF THE ESSENCE AND ALL TRACTORS ARE OTHER-WISE IN USE, BRUTE FORCE IS USED TO GET A "CLEAR DECK" RAPIDLY. HERE, THE VARIOUS PERSONNEL UNITE TO GET THE JOB DONE, POSITIONING AN F/A-18 HORNET AS CLOSE TO THE EDGE OF THE DECK AS POSSIBLE WITHOUT LOSING THE PLANE OVER THE SIDE—A POSSIBILITY THAT COULD BECOME REAL WERE A SUDDEN RUDDER MOVEMENT TO BE MADE OR AN UNEXPECTED ROLL TO OCCUR.

ABOVE, ON THE *KITTY HAWK*, A DIRECTOR
POSITIONS AN F/A-18 HORNET ON THE CATA-
PULT AS OTHER MEMBERS OF THE FLIGHT-
DECK TEAM STAND READY TO HOOK UP THE
AIRCRAFT FOR LAUNCH.

OPPOSITE, A DIRECTOR—A "YELLOW
SHIRT"—SIGNALS WHAT MOVEMENTS THE
PILOT SHOULD MAKE TO POSITION THE AIR-
CRAFT FOR HOOKUP ON THE CATAPULT.

OPPOSITE, ON THE SIGNAL OF THE *KITTY HAWK'S* CATAPULT OFFICER, A GREEN-SHIRTED DECK-EDGE OPERATOR ON THE CATWALK ACTUALLY FIRES THE CATAPULT SENDING THIS F-14 TOMCAT OFF IN A BLURRING 150-KNOT LAUNCH.

BELOW, THE CATAPULT CREW "HOLD-BACK MAN" ATTACHES A HOLD-BACK UNIT TO AN F-14 TOMCAT. THE UNIT WILL HOLD THE PLANE IN PLACE UNTIL A PRESCRIBED FORCE BREAKS THE UNIT, RELEASING THE PLANE TO MOVE DOWN THE CATAPULT WITH THE SHUTTLE.

ABOVE, AS HE GOES TO FULL POWER WITH HIS JET ENGINES, AN F-14 TOMCAT PILOT SALUTES THE CATAPULT OFFICER, THE FINAL STEP IN SIGNIFYING HIS READINESS FOR LAUNCH.

wire in the landing area as it retracts, using a five-foot steel bar. Deck checkers make sure the landing area is FOD-free and that the wires are in proper position for aircraft recovery and that personnel are clear of the landing area. Recovery-equipment operators coordinate the setting of the arresting gear and visual landing aids with below-decks personnel, and photographers—also "green shirts"—photograph and videotape flight ops for documentation and for PR purposes.

The scramble you saw a few minutes ago was caused by a blown tire on an A-6 that was landing. The "green shirts" who changed the tire so fast were from the squadron maintenance crew—their jerseys are marked with a squadron designator and a black stripe front and back. Down in the hangar deck right now there's a FOD'ed engine being changed by "green shirts," and the man making the final inspection—checking the entire job—is wearing a white jersey with a black checkered pattern.

LSO—LANDING SIGNALS OFFICER

The first thing to know when you're standing up here on the LSO platform is that it can be a very, very dangerous place during recovery operations. There's an LSO from each squadron up here, grading

ABOVE, AN F-14 TOMCAT IN AFTERBURNER, AT FULL POWER, AT THE MOMENT OF DEPARTING THE DECK.

PREVIOUS PAGE, VIEWED FROM BEHIND THE AIRCRAFT, THE INTENSE HEAT AND POWER OF THE F-14 TOMCAT IN AFTERBURNER AT THE MOMENT OF CATAPULT LAUNCH DISTORTS THE LIGHT RAYS PASSING TO THE CAMERA. IN OTHER PARTS OF THE FLIGHT DECK AND HANGAR DECK, MAINTENANCE PETTY OFFICER "GREEN SHIRTS" RAPIDLY REMOVE A WORN ARRESTING-GEAR CABLE, REPLACE AN "FOD'ED" ENGINE ON AN A-6 INTRUDER, AND CHANGE A BLOWN-OUT TIRE ON ANOTHER A-6 THAT HAD JUST LANDED.

67

CITY AT SEA

"traps" and staying ready to assist with his planes—with you and those two "green shirts," that makes about ten of us trying to dive over the side into that so-called safety net one deck below. If a plane looks like it's going to hit the edge, we'll be going over like a herd of lemmings. Don't look too closely at that net—those eight-inch steel stanchions outside and under it make you think that the impact would brain you or at best break some bones, especially "piling on," but I guess that's better than being chopped and burned by the crash!

I make sure that the aircraft stays within safe parameters during its approach and have to make sure that the deck is clear for its landing, otherwise I signal a "waveoff"—which means he has to go around again. The pilot's flying on a glide path that if flown perfectly will have him catching the third wire. He's "flying the ball," changing his power in tiny increments and adjusting to stay on centerline. You can hear the "rrrrhhh, rrrrhhhh" of the engines as he applies a little throttle or cuts power a little. I can talk to him on the radio—you just heard me repeating, "Power, power" to that last one—he was staying a bit low, and he would have seen that the "ball"—the yellow light—was below the green line of lights. If I see he's out of the envelope, I'll signal a waveoff, and he'll see a row of red lights. But if he's on glide path, he hits the deck at about 140 miles per hour and goes to full power just in case his tailhook misses all the wires—that's the only way he can have enough speed to make it off the deck; otherwise, he's in the water.

"PURPLE SHIRTS"—THE "GRAPES"

I'm the flight-deck fuels chief, and I work directly for the fuels officer. He's responsible for fueling and defueling all of our aircraft as well as for the operation of the fuel system and pumps and filters, and also for the catapult lube-oil system. I'm responsible for the training and supervision of the flight-deck fueling crew, the "grapes" as we call them. They handle all fueling and defueling of the aircraft from fueling stations located around the flight and hangar decks. See those guys dragging out the fuel hoses over there? They're "grapes," about to top off that helo that just landed. They're pulling the hoses and nozzles out now, then they'll stick them in the bird and turn on the fuel. You'll see the same guys in a few minutes giving more fuel to those T-2s with training pilots making their first carrier landings. On an average day we'll refuel about 140 to 150 aircraft, and we average fourteen to sixteen hours a day. The air boss and handler pass the word down to us about how much fuel we have to put in to keep them flying for the number of cat shots and traps they need, and they watch us like hawks to see that the job is right and safe. Daytime is just hard work; night can be petrifying! Total attention is the rule; even so there are slips and falls on wet or oily decks.

RIGHT, ON A HAZY DAY, AN F/A-18 HORNET OBSERVES A "FOUL DECK" AND PASSES BY THE CARRIER TO MAKE ANOTHER APPROACH TO THE SHIP.

BELOW, ANOTHER HORNET MAKES A PERFECT LANDING ON THE *SARATOGA.*

OPPOSITE, ON A FIERCE AND STORMY DAY, WITH THE WINDCHILL FACTOR BRINGING THE TEMPERATURE BELOW MINUS THIRTY DEGREES BELOW ZERO, "SEA SMOKE" RISES FROM THE SALT OCEAN WATERS OFF NORFOLK, VIRGINIA. AN E-2C HAWKEYE RECONNAISSANCE AIRCRAFT HEELS SHARPLY UPON LANDING ON THE USS *GEORGE WASHINGTON* BECAUSE OF TRICKY AND UNPREDICTABLE GUSTS OF WIND.

LEFT, THE LSO PLATFORM DURING THE RECOVERY OF AIRCRAFT. REPRESENTATIVES FROM EACH SQUADRON ARE PRESENT TO BOTH GRADE LANDINGS AND TO ASSIST IN BRINGING PLANES ABOARD.

A PURPLE-SHIRTED AVIATION-FUELS SPECIAL-
IST, NICKNAMED A "GRAPE," CARRIES A
FUELING HOSE TO AN AIRCRAFT THAT HAS
JUST LANDED AND REQUIRES FUEL.

OPPOSITE, ON BOARD THE *KITTY HAWK*,
A STUDENT PILOT HAS JUST LANDED A TA-4J
TRAINER. FUELING PERSONNEL, THE "GRAPES,"
RAPIDLY REFUEL THE AIRCRAFT, EMPLOYING
THE LOWEST GRADE OF TECHNOLOGY IN AN
ASSISTING ROLE—A COMMON KITCHEN MOP.

"RED SHIRTS"—SQUADRON ORDNANCE PETTY OFFICER

The weapons people—the "red shirts"—up here on the flight deck are a mixture of air wing people and ship's force. These loading ordnance on the aircraft are ours—the squadron's and wing's. We're with the ship when the air wing comes aboard, and we leave when the wing leaves. Back there by the weapons elevator that's bringing up those missiles, those are ship's force. Their jerseys don't have black unit designators on them. Down in the magazine—way down—the ship's force weps [weapons] guys assemble the weapons that they send up to us for loading. Modern technology is great in giving us weapons that are from smart to brilliant, but it hasn't done a damned thing to help us in the mule-hauling work of marrying ordnance to airplane. Arnold Schwarzenneger must have been a bomb loader in his first life! Look at those young guys straining with that iron bomb! Just imagine having to do that when the ship is rolling and the decks are wet! Supervisors have to be on them like a blanket—it's no picnic!

ORDNANCE-HANDLING OFFICER

You might say that our people in red shirts and the ordnance they assemble and move is the whole reason we have this carrier and all the aircraft. The final product is ordnance on target, isn't it? We have a sizable force of ordnance specialists who almost never see the light of day—they live deep down in the magazines for twelve-hour shifts—if you're talking about a "city at sea," then I guess these fellows are the rats, living as they do. They get their requirements from load plans from Ordnance Control and put the necessary types of bombs and missiles together. Some of it is fine, detailed work; some is just plain dog work. A number of two hundred to near three hundred isn't too unusual in a day. From the magazine, weapons are moved topside by weapons elevators and then to the "bomb farm" on the starboard side of the island, then to the squadron ordnance handlers—the "B-B stackers"—and onto the planes. We arm them just before takeoff, and if they aren't expended, we "safe" them right after the plane gets clear of the wire area.

Obviously, safety is a number one concern. Probably every safety precaution in the book originated with some horrible accident. The men who do this work in the magazine have to go through a tough qualification and certification, including exams by an oral board made up of department officers. We also have our EOD [explosive ordnance disposal] officer and crew who disarm, safe, or get rid of defective weapons. Those "red shirts" have "EOD" on the front and back. Then, while you don't see their red shirts much because they're covered by special silver fire-fighting suits, we have our "crash" crews—the flight-deck fire department.

BELOW, RED-SHIRTED WEAPONS SPECIALISTS STRAIN WITH THE EFFORT OF HOLDING A 500-POUND BOMB IN POSITION WHILE LOADING IT ON AN F/A-18 HORNET.

LEFT, A WEAPONS SPECIALIST, A "RED SHIRT," LOADS A SIDEWINDER MISSILE ON AN F/A-18 HORNET.

RIGHT, ON BOARD THE USS *GEORGE WASHINGTON,* WEAPONS SPECIALISTS LOAD ORDNANCE ON AN F/A-18 HORNET.

BELOW, THE HEAVY-ORDNANCE-CARRYING CAPACITY OF THE A-6 INTRUDER IS EVIDENT AS WEAPONS SPECIALISTS LOAD THE AIRCRAFT.

"WHITE SHIRTS"—SAFETY OFFICER

My job is safety officer. I, along with the others who are basically safety involved, wear white jerseys, usually with some large print or insignia that shows a special category. For example, in a mass casualty, when we simulate a catastrophe and lots of wounded, you will see chaplains and doctors conducting triage, treatment, counseling, and such. The doctors and their corpsmen will wear white jerseys with a red cross. The chaplain will wear white with block letters "Chaplain." A very special white shirt is the LSO, who wears a white shirt with block "LSO" on it. He's stationed port side aft during recovery ops. The air transport officer—ATO—and his men who handle the loading and unloading of air cargo from the COD as well as passengers wear white shirts. Just about any time we have flight ops you'll notice a white jersey somewhere around, maybe not right in the flail like the yellow or green guys, but on the fringes, keeping an eye on the whole evolution, ready to check and stop anything that looks a little careless or is getting on the ragged edge of proper procedure.

The squadrons have a number of highly trained sailors who are plane inspectors. They are "final checkers," sometimes called "shooters" for "troubleshooters"—not to be confused with the "shooter" who is the catapult officer. You can tell them by the black-and-white checkerboard on the front and back of their shirts, with squadron or wing designators and green helmets. One of them was just here checking that tire replacement on the A-6, and if you go down to the hangar deck right now you'll probably see one near that FOD'ed motor change. The final checker is responsible for the physical safety and inspection of aircraft just prior to launch.

To sum it all up, all of us live, eat, dream, and sleep safety. No other way!

OPPOSITE, MAINTENANCE PERSONNEL ARE ASSISTED BY A SAFETY TROUBLESHOOTER DURING CHECKS OF AN SH-3H SEA KING HELICOPTER ON THE *GEORGE WASHINGTON.*

BELOW, A WHITE-SHIRTED SAFETY OFFICER WATCHES MAINTENANCE PERSONNEL DURING AN AT-SEA REPLACEMENT OF A DAMAGED A-6 JET ENGINE ON BOARD THE USS *KITTY HAWK.*

AIRCRAFT SQUADRON COMMANDER

You're looking at a real success story—the way 5,500 guys from all over the country and with all different backgrounds can get it together and make an aircraft carrier and air wing just sing! As a pilot, I'm getting up in time to where catting off and trapping so many times a day doesn't give me the thrill as when I was a "jaygee" [lieutenant junior grade], but I love flying. I'm probably a hell of a lot more conservative now—a lot more careful—I don't have to prove to anyone that I'm a "good stick" [good pilot, especially at flying the ball down to a trap]. I see myself in so many of the new pilots—some better, some worse. They come in all bright-eyed and just bubble over about flying off the boat. Go to the wardroom when they come in from a night trap—they're loud, laugh at anything, jump around spontaneously "high-fiving"—they're really "pumped up" with adrenalin. I worry a little when they get hit with the fact that the Navy's forced to cut back—that we're telling pilots with sixteen years in "Bam! Bam! Thank you, ma'am!" It's tough!

For them, it's the "fun life" now. It'll be a few years before they feel that there are only so many seats up above. Some things are screwed up today by the Navy trying to cope with programs forced on us—like needing to have "joint" duty, which squashes your senior career so that a guy can be a CAG or command a carrier, but not both. And a limit of eighteen months in command—when a lot of that might be in a "yard"—dumb! We'd probably be a lot better off if we'd just let some fly and some run ships *really* well—not just getting checkoffs—until they die or retire, rather than trying to make them all admirals or CNO! My "flyer" philosophy!

Sometimes young pilots forget that they're not the only working hands on board, and they have to stop to think about it—but all of us come to realize pretty quick that we'd be doodly-squat if we didn't have all of those 5,500 keeping us flying and alive. Sure, we do check our own aircraft, but there's only so much we can get to. Our lives and our planes are in the hands of those guys who check the fuel, who fix the tires, who inspect the wires, who set the weights, who are ready to put out the fires, get us to our spots, keep us from rolling overboard—some eighteen to nineteen years old, some fifty—they all do a hell of a job! When I trap in a snowstorm, or rough weather at night—or when windchill is way below zero—man, I do thank God for all of them. A lot of them risk life and limb every hour. We do appreciate it!

CAPTAIN, REMINISCING

This is maybe the most unforgettable experience in the life of those guys circling around us—they'll remember it all the rest of their lives. Their first "trap"—arrested landing on board a carrier! Really, their

AN F-14 TOMCAT PILOT AND RADAR INTERCEPT OFFICER JUST PRIOR TO MOVING UP TO POSITION ON THE CATAPULT FOR LAUNCH.

LT JOHN SUMMERS
ROWDY

first *night* carrier landing might be tougher, or at least their first night landing in a blowing storm when the deck's pitching—but I absolutely guarantee they'll never forget the first one they make today! These students are flying those trainers now by themselves and until today have never approached a carrier—never really have come to grips with how small that deck really is! It really gets you nervous. You see guys making the trap, then being almost "out of it"—you know, not cutting the engine when signaled, being slow to follow the director's hand signals, things like that.

Now, we've given each student three "touch-and-go's"—their tailhook's not even down—so they get the feel of what it's like. They've done pretty well. Tell you—I remember my own first one so-o-o well! I made it—hooked the second wire—and then almost couldn't taxi clear of the landing area! My knees were actually knocking together—awful—for some time. Then, I taxied to the parking spot, cut the engine, and looked up—and there was the Captain staring right down at me! Steely eyes just boring in! I felt like shrinking down to the pedals. Unforgettable!

Here comes the first one—nice—small corrections—third wire

ABOVE, **ON BOARD THE** *SARATOGA,* **AN A-6 PILOT COMPLETES THE NOT-INSIGNIFICANT CHORE OF DONNING FULL FLIGHT REGALIA AS FLIGHT QUARTERS ARE MANNED.**

FOLLOWING PAGE, **A MEMORABLE OCCASION FOR THE STUDENT PILOT IN THE T-2 BUCKEYE TRAINER IS HIS FIRST SUCCESSFUL CARRIER LANDING ON THE** *KITTY HAWK.* **NOW IF THEY CAN ONLY GET THE EXCITED YOUNG PILOT TO RAISE THE TAILHOOK!**

ABOVE, F/A-18 HORNETS AND AN S-3 VIKING ON
THE FLIGHT DECK OF THE *SARATOGA*.

A HIGHLIGHT FOR ANY AIRCRAFT CARRIER OR ANY
SHIP IS THE FIRST BUILDER'S TRIALS, WHEN THE
SHIP GOES TO SEA AND IS TESTED FOR THE FIRST
TIME. THE USS *GEORGE WASHINGTON* ON
BUILDER'S TRIALS IN THE ATLANTIC OCEAN. (U.S.
NAVY PHOTO, PH1 JOHNNY BEVER)

trap—great! Look—he didn't raise the tailhook on signal—see what I mean? Now they've got to him. Clear! Here comes the next guy—nice approach—down! Third wire! Hell, these guys are better than the air wing!

EMBARKED WOMAN VISITOR, LOOKING DOWN ON THE FLIGHT DECK

This is such a thrilling experience! Our group of older—pardon me, *senior*—women are all former pilots who ferried planes over the "Hump" in World War II. Now, to experience a carrier landing and catapult takeoff from a carrier at sea is really the icing on the cake! The planes we flew were like kids' toys compared to these! Looking down on the flight deck from up here on "Vulture's Row"—the noise of the jet engines is overwhelming—the heat blasts you even up here. The whole thing's about power! They talk about how the whole flight-deck scene is a ballet in motion—it is that—and so colorful! All of those different colors of jerseys scampering about—all I can think of is spilling a bag of M&M's!

IN A CEREMONY AVAILABLE ONLY IN AIRCRAFT

CARRIERS, THE NORMALLY "SPIT AND POLISH"

RENDERING OF HONORS TO DISTINGUISHED

GUESTS FEATURES "RAINBOW SIDEBOYS,"

SAILORS IN EACH DISTINCTIVE WORKING

UNIFORM OF THE FLIGHT-DECK CREW.

FOLLOWING PAGE, FIRST CRACK OF DAWN

FINDS THE USS *KITTY HAWK* MAKING AN

APPROACH TO THE OILER *GUADALUPE* FOR

AN UNDERWAY REPLENISHMENT, OR

"UNREP."

ABOVE, BAKERS ON BOARD THE USS *GEORGE WASHINGTON* HAVE A FULL-TIME JOB AT SEA IN MEETING THE NEEDS OF 5,500 CREW AND AIR WING MEMBERS.

RIGHT, IN CENTRAL CONTROL OF THE ENGINEERING SPACES, ENGINEERING WATCH STANDERS OF THE *KITTY HAWK* RESPOND TO SPEED AND POWER REQUIREMENTS AS SIGNALED FROM THE BRIDGE.

OPPOSITE, TOP, CREW'S BERTHING OF THE USS
GEORGE WASHINGTON APPEARS LUXURIOUS COM-
PARED TO THAT OF SHIPS OF A BYGONE DAY.
BELOW, MANY DECKS BELOW THE FLIGHT DECK,
WEAPONS SPECIALISTS, THE "RED SHIRTS," OF
THE USS KITTY HAWK ASSEMBLE BOMBS.

THE SQUADRON READY ROOMS OF THE GEORGE
WASHINGTON PROVIDE AN AREA FOR THE PILOTS
TO RELAX, GRAB A CUP OF COFFEE, CONVERSE,
HOLD OPERATIONAL AND INTELLIGENCE BRIEFINGS,
COMPLETE POST-FLIGHT REPORTS, OR EVEN STEAL
A MOMENT FOR WRITING A QUICK LETTER.

THE CREW

The two visitors to a carrier indoctrination cruise have turned in early and are soon snoring after a long, tiring day of repeatedly climbing ladders and watching flight operations. As VIPs, their status has earned them a relatively private stateroom with head and shower adjacent. As they found their room, they chortled at the facilities—they felt *lucky*. Well, the two VIPs are *unlucky*—their convenient stateroom is in the after part of the ship—in fact, directly under the landing strip! Only the thickness of the flight deck separates them from the aircraft catching a wire above their heads. So "zeroed-in" are they that they are interrupted by two electricians bent upon restoring one of the centerline lights—right in their ceiling—that had malfunctioned. Light restored, they resume "Zs."

Ker-flumpt! The impact of thirty-four tons of F-14 Tomcat a foot or two above their heads virtually fractures their eyeballs!

Sleep now impossible, they turn on the TV monitor and assess the quality of landings and hold their own recognition class on aircraft types, correlating with the noise of impact. The "heavy" is the F-14, the F/A-18 a bit lighter; the S-3 almost "kisses" the deck and could be "sleepable"—maybe. A bolter for any type makes a shattering "crack," an unmistakable noise. Flight ops for the day complete, they hit the sack with a vengeance.

They have just fallen asleep again when the 1-MC announcing system crackles, a boatswain's pipe whistles, and they hear, "All hands, stand by for the evening prayer!" Obviously, the liberal non-school-prayer people haven't torpedoed the Navy! After the chaplain has given his short prayer, tailored to the day's events, it's back to dreamville until a few hours have passed, when the odious 1-MC raucously crackles a host of terms that baffle the visitors: "Reveille! Reveille! Up all

OPPOSITE, **ON BOARD THE USS *KITTY HAWK* DURING A BRIEF MOORING IN SAN DIEGO TO OFF-LOAD AIR WING PERSONNEL AND EQUIPMENT, DIVISIONS OF THE SHIP'S CREW MUSTER AT QUARTERS ON THE FLIGHT DECK PRIOR TO GETTING UNDER WAY.**

hands!" They understand that, but come to breakfast asking the meaning of such as "Sweepers! Sweepers!" or "Heave to, trice up!" and other terms that fell upon drowsy ears. Hey! Isn't that the "Old Navy"? But these visitors now have a taste of the hardships that surround a sailor daily on a busy carrier! A full night's sleep is a gift of the gods.

Technology has exploded upon weapons systems, ships, and aircraft. The advances of the past few decades leave not only civilian visitors but also seasoned veterans gasping in disbelief. But the common denominator of their awe and respect is the performance of the people—the crews of the Navy's ships. Somewhere, somehow, there must be a limit as to how much more technology, information, sleeplessness, and personal sacrifice can be placed upon those who choose to compete in a naval environment. Imagine—for many, their wages for all of this are less than they made as teenagers working in Roy Rogers or Wendy's! Watching the crews, though, one ventures to guess that we haven't yet reached the "knee of the curve" on what to expect from young sailors—except on the count of separation from family. That factor at least has gone beyond the good of the Navy, and further demands are ill-advised (barring manning the ships with the policy-makers who cause the need). On the other factors, they rise to the challenge and seem to signal, "More!"

As the visitors perceived, much remains of the "Old Navy," but a lot has had to change to assure a continuity in crew manning. Young people today have many more choices. They have to see accomplishment and reward; they have to understand "why"; they expect to ask questions, and to receive answers. The tenets of leadership haven't changed, only the manner of implementation has softened in a nod to the march of time and values. "People" is both word and concept, firmly ingrained in the minds of the leadership echelons, and the Captain, the executive officer, the command master chief, and the department and division leaders devote a significant portion of each day to paying attention to their people.

Two examples that occurred during the research for this book leap to mind, each having a common root—the national preoccupation with sports, football in particular—and each demonstrating a captain's sensitivity to the loves of his crew. In the first, the carrier was steaming off southern California on the Saturday of the Army-Navy Game, and flight operations for the day were not scheduled for several hours. The Captain had left the bridge to visit a space below-decks, where he noted sailors frantically trying to draw a meaningful signal from the static on their TV. Picking up the phone, he asked, "Do you have any ship contacts in sight?" On getting a negative reply, he directed the officer of the deck to start changing course slowly, until, watching the TV, he saw the reception boom in clearly. "That's it! Steer that course!" was his order.

In a closely related incident, another carrier was en route to Puerto Rico on a Sunday when an NFL Super Bowl playoff game was being broadcast. No flight ops were scheduled. Far from direct reception range, the ship was attempting to receive the game on a newly installed satellite antenna. The Captain had gone on record to assure the crew that they would see the game. Ha! He had not reckoned with the technicality that on the southerly course the structures high up on the island blocked the antenna, providing a screen of "snow" in lieu of a game. Undaunted, he, too, attempted changing the ship's course to see if better reception might be gained. Unfortunately, he was required by schedule to make good progress toward Puerto Rico, and the only course that provided good (in fact, flawless) reception was the reverse of his track—heading back to Norfolk! Someone on the bridge wondered *if*—perhaps *if*—the ship's propellers were reversed, the ship

could make stern way and successfully steer a straight course toward its goal. Ah! Flexibility! They could, and they did! Not at full speed, but good speed nonetheless. A commanding voice came over the announcing system: "This is the Captain. Some time ago I promised you guys that we'd see the playoffs. OK! We found that the only course we could receive the game on was heading 180 from where we're heading. This is probably the first time in history that a ship has backed to Puerto Rico!" Queried on the bridge after the game, he responded with a broad grin, "I'd be damned if I was going back on my promise and disappoint six thousand guys if I could help it!"

The chaplain's evening prayer that night demonstrated an awareness of just what counts to a crew, who listened attentively with grins: "Through the marvelous medium of satellite and TV technology, Lord, and the thoughtful cooperation of those driving this magnificent ship, football fans could watch the playoff contests of the NFL. As with the contests of life that we all experience, O God, there was exuberant celebration and disappointing defeats. But we are thankful that you still encourage us to rise above our disappointments and not to get complacent when we rack up victories. As the proud *George Washington* crew and air wing, help us constantly to improve where we have needs, and to remember humbly that our successes are your blessings. May we be individually faithful in the contests of our life, so that we will be found to be winners in your sight in the Super Bowl of heaven. . . ."

Leadership! (Parenthetically, and not just coincidentally, *both* of these captains were selected to the rank of rear admiral by the very next Navy flag selection board! It's called "caring.")

The busy gyrations of the flight- and hangar-deck crews are the principal focus of visitors to a carrier. They and the entire air operation are "front page" news: the catapults, and aircraft roaring off the ship; the arresting gear, and aircraft "trapping"; air-traffic controllers directing the air pattern; an entire off-watch crew walking the flight deck en masse in a "FOD walkdown" to pick up extraneous matter and forestall a damaged jet engine. Less apparent but no less occupied are thousands who "make the ship go" and perform other necessary tasks ranging from cleaning heads to cleaning teeth. Scores of people who are seldom seen perform important functions continuously. Watch standers in an obscure space called "steering aft" provide an emergency capability for steering the ship in the event of steering casualty. The pump rooms, festooned with networks of piping painted in the lavender hue designating jet fuel, are the kingdom of pump operators who transfer the fuel to a number of stations and of technicians who assure the quality of the fuel going to the aircraft. Critical to the catapulting and trapping of aircraft are the sailors standing watch in two rooms where the

OPPOSITE, IN A LULL BETWEEN FLIGHT OPERATIONS, THE CAPTAIN OF THE *KITTY HAWK* JOGS ON AN UNUSUALLY BRIGHT AND SUNNY DAY. THE F-14 TOMCAT BEHIND HIM SUFFERED A MAJOR CASUALTY DURING THE DEPLOYMENT FOLLOWING THIS AT-SEA PERIOD. ON LANDING, THE AIRCRAFT STRUCK THE APRON AT THE STERN; THE PILOT AND RADAR INTERCEPT OFFICER EJECTED, AND THE PLANE WAS TOTALLY DESTROYED BY FIRE ON THE FLIGHT DECK. HEROICALLY, THE CRASH CREW RESCUED THE PILOT SECONDS AFTER HIS PARACHUTE DELIVERED HIM INTO THE CENTER OF THE FIREBALL. *BELOW,* OFF-WATCH CREW MEMBERS SCAN THE FLIGHT DECK TO CLEAN IT OF ANY OBJECTS THAT MIGHT BE PICKED UP BY JET ENGINE

noise of huge valves and equipment is so great that hearing can be permanently impaired without double ear protection. The engineering spaces, without which the ship would be little more than a floating steel island, are difficult to access, or in the case of nuclear-powered ships are "out of bounds" for security reasons. And so much more.

Examine the makeup of a modern carrier crew. First off, it's a microcosm of America, with roots in every state and religion. Diversity personified, it becomes more so with the full implementation of programs incorporating women in combat ships. Caucasians make up about 77 percent, African Americans 21 to 22 percent, Asian Americans about 0.5 percent, and Native Americans about 0.2 to 0.3 percent, a mix thoroughly sifted and spread evenly among all departments of the ship. The size of departments or divisions gives a clue to the size of its task—but only a clue. For example, the ship exists to fly its air wing, yet the cutting edge is the group of pilots, NFOs, and aircrewmen numbering about 250. The remainder of air wing personnel supporting the maintenance and administrative efforts of the aircraft squadrons comes to about 2,200.

In the ship's force, a rough allocation of major functions follows: hangar- and flight-deck crews, over 600, and major aircraft maintenance, 240; Engineering and Reactor Departments, over 400 each; weapons handlers, over 200. The supply officer has about 250 food-service people to handle the massive job of cooking and feeding, and about an additional 200 for pay, accounting, running a ship's store, and ensuring a ready barrage of well-stocked spare-parts shelves. The First Lieutenant ensures the readiness and handling of boats as well as the mooring of the ship dockside and any underway replenishments with a Deck Department of 150. One hundred and forty electronic technicians care for the complex equipment, while some 30 quartermasters and signalmen assist the navigator in getting the ship where it's supposed to be without running aground. The entire medical and dental needs of a crew of this size falls to a Medical Department of some 65 to 70, who handle everything from tooth fillings to major surgery with continuing care. Thirty air traffic controllers handle the stressful task of keeping the flight patterns safe during the hectic spasms of landings, takeoffs, refuelings, and emergencies, while 120 to 140 skilled operators conduct the often complex business of separating friendly contacts from hostile or neutral and fighting the battle in the Combat Direction Center. Not last—and *never, ever* least—a platoon-size detachment of marines provides security-related tasks.

Now, last, some 300 enlisted personnel and officers round out the crew in a number of smaller divisions that play a major role in the ship's success. For example, a typical Public Affairs Division of ten people handles the press and visitors, an extremely important task in assuring that policymakers and John Q. Public alike have accurate

OFFICER ROOMMATES RELAX IN A TWO-MAN STATEROOM ON THE *GEORGE WASHINGTON*.

knowledge of the carrier's capabilities. In one year, for example, one busy ship had 150 organized tours or at-sea embarkations totaling 9,000 visitors! The public affairs folks also provide special programs for the ship's closed-circuit TV and put out the ship's daily newspaper printed by—don't forget them—the print shop, with photos from, of course, a well-manned and -equipped photo lab. Looking at other small divisions—who would want to forget the Parachute Loft? And let's not overlook those small "cubbyholes" where sailors control or maintain the defensive systems—the Sea Sparrow missiles or Close-in Weapons System.

The driving challenge for the entire crew is to become well-trained for flight ops whenever they are conducted, but if an emphasis is placed on any part of a cycle of operations, it is on the deployment—a six-month period when the ship and its air wing are maintained in either the Far East, the Middle East, or the Mediterranean Sea. Continuous operation far from the support of Stateside echelons, daily operations within a battle group, a frequently changing operating locale, and the knowledge that at any time they may be on a battle footing against a variety of hostile threats keep a sharp edge on the readiness and training of the entire crew. For a septuagenarian, six months seem to fly by—not so for an eighteen to twenty-five year old! While some bachelors may relish a schedule of foreign port visits to "see the world," six months is a long, long time for young married sailors. The "great job" they are doing "showing the flag" and "keeping the lid on" provide only temporary salve for the wounds of separation from girlfriend, wife, or family. Deployment tests the mettle of the ship's leadership at all echelons.

Competent leaders realize the need for "breaks" to ease what can become monotony in even the busiest of operations. A fantastic aircraft

sortie rate keeps the juices running for the Captain, pilots, and the Air Department, but it does little to spice up the life of a machinist's mate deep within the ship, nor of the brig guard, or the cook or baker who does the same thing hour-by-hour, day-by-day, hamburger-by-hamburger. On a routine basis, during any type of operation, the crew has access to first-line movies and taped videos, computer games, and well-equipped workout and weight rooms. Some take advantage of the Program for Afloat College Education (PACE) with classes conducted by civilian instructors embarked aboard the ship. The leadership in our carriers, aware of the added pressures of deployment, exercises imagination in scheduling meaningful foreign port visits, educational tours of historic places, and recreational activities ashore or on board. Some, while at anchor, provide a "play day" on the flight deck, when a shipboard version of a neighborhood picnic takes place—various competitions, makeshift band concerts, races, team games, and even pie-eating contests. Another imaginative feature is a "running the ditch" contest for runners conducted while a ship transits the Suez Canal. Some have succeeded in telephoning their families through Sprint telephones or amateur radio facilities. Modern technology helps, but it doesn't bring the deployed sailor home.

The happiest day during the deployment of the carrier—or of any ship—is that day when it arrives back in home port. The wife of a family deprived of a male presence for so long has started a flurry of housecleaning several weeks in advance; the children talk more and more of daddy's being home; toys get picked up with less urging. The wife, a bit tired of hearing only those tiny voices, anticipates the sound of a mature, happy male voice. On the wonderful day, new and colorful dresses and suits abound. Bright umbrellas barely protect young and old from a heavy rain that dampens clothes but not spirits! Tiny voices babble, others laugh or squeal, and anticipation and excitement is infectious as "the boat" rounds a point and becomes visible in the mist! Wives, kids, moms, dads, grandparents, "just friends"—yes, and husbands—carry colorful signs proclaiming, "Welcome home." Even a small white poodle, obviously an "only child" in the arms of one beaming "mother," whines—happily oblivious to the grins and head shakes of nearby greeters amused at the perky sailor suit and tasseled sailor beret his mistress has picked for the occasion! The whole waterfront knows it! They're back!

COMMAND MASTER CHIEF

I'm the senior enlisted adviser to the Captain and executive officer, and one of my major jobs is to focus the efforts of the leading chief petty officers of all departments of the ship. In this modern Navy, people have a tendency to try to jump over steps in the chain of command

A SEASONED LEADING ORDNANCE PETTY OFFICER WATCHES CLOSELY AS HIS CREW LOADS WEAPONS ON AN AIRCRAFT. SUCH LEADERS ARE THE LIFEBLOOD OF AN EFFECTIVE CREW.

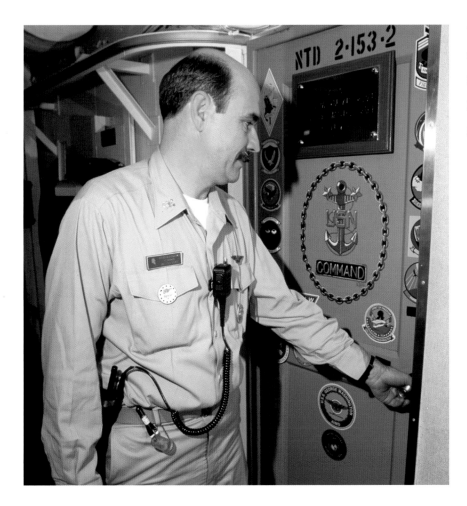

THE COMMAND MASTER CHIEF, THE SENIOR
ENLISTED MAN IN THE CREW AND A LEAD-
ING ADVISER TO THE CAPTAIN, RETURNS TO
HIS OFFICE AFTER TOURING THE *GEORGE
WASHINGTON*'S LIVING SPACES.

101

CITY AT SEA

and get right to the top with their own personal idea of how to run a leave schedule, liberty, ship's operations, or with what they see as their private, unique problem. When I talk to some of the real "Old Navy" chiefs—guys retired and in their sixties or seventies—they always talk about how it was "much better then": you know, "marlinespike leadership," the attitude that "a wife didn't come in your seabag," those types of things. They laugh when I tell them that we have a different sailor now than what they knew—or when I say that today's sailor is a much more focused person, has more choices, and is more educated and worldly, on average.

Of course, people see me as "the old chief." Hell, I'm just a kid who enlisted just as the Navy permitted beards and came up with ombudsmen. I grew up in the Navy in the era of "paying attention to people." It makes good sense to me to listen to people's problems, and not to dismiss what they think they need as a petty annoyance. The world's changed, and the Navy's changed with it. I'll listen to any sailor and his problems or suggestions. I had a lot of ideas to air out as I came up, and some of them worked out so well that here I am, an E-9. My office has an open door all the time. I do expect, though, that a man will have taken his problem to his leading petty officer and to his chief before I get into it too much, and I'd like to know that his division officer has gotten into it before we start making something major about it.

OPPOSITE, THE NUCLEAR AIRCRAFT CARRIER
USS *GEORGE WASHINGTON* AT ANCHOR OFF
PONCE, PUERTO RICO, PROVIDING A VISIT
AND EXTENSIVE PROGRAM OF TOURS BY
SHIP'S PERSONNEL DURING A BREAK IN RIG-
OROUS TRAINING EXERCISES.

One of the things we do here is "Captain's call," when the Captain, the XO, and I are on our closed-circuit TV to pass the word on policy or schedules, or on things happening on the ship. At sea we do this each week, and it's scheduled in advance. We invite written questions from the crew and answer them on TV. That way, the whole crew gets to see and know the leadership more. You know, the ship's so big that some people only see us occasionally, even though the three of us make it a point to visit hard-to-get-to spaces some parts of each week. I really believe that our officers and chiefs work at the leadership thing very well, and I think anyone watching our crew at work, at flight quarters, at UNREP [underway replenishment], or going on liberty, will have to say that our attention to people has paid off. I don't want to sound off too much, but we're good!

DIVISION OFFICER, COMBAT DIRECTION CENTER

Our space, CDC, is the nerve center of the ship. It takes about fifty people, officer and enlisted, headed by a tactical action officer (TAO), on watch for twenty-four hours a day when at sea to support the Captain and embarked staffs and to protect the ship from attack. We play a key role in maintaining command and control of modern-day naval warfare. We work with five modules—antisurface, antisubmarine, electronic warfare, air detection and tracking, and air warfare—each having distinct functions that play together to give us control of the tactical picture in a very big area of ocean. Basically, each module works the field its name suggests, detecting ships, aircraft, subs, and electronic signals and doing something about it. Once a detection is made, the contact is tracked and its course and speed solved to permit a targeting solution should engagement be necessary. Each module uses information from all sources; for example, the surface picture may be fed by our radars, by radars or visual from aircraft, or other ships or submarines. The ASW [antisubmarine warfare] module uses inputs from our own ASW aircraft and its sonobuoys, but also those from the entire battle group, including our submarines. So, in a nutshell, CDC collects, evaluates, displays, and disseminates tactical information, feeding it up the line to the decision makers.

The surface module has a subset called the tactical operational plot located aft of the bridge on the 09-level in the island, which is run by the surface-watch officer. It assists the officer of the deck with tactical maneuvers, navigation, and piloting the ship in restricted water. The track supervisor is the "honcho" of the air-detection-and-tracking module, which monitors the air-search radars, and he also manages the Navy Tactical Data Link [which automatically and electronically shares target data] between ships and aircraft, keeping the whole battle group

OPPOSITE, A PLANE CAPTAIN AND WEAPONS TECHNICIANS TAKE A BREAK AFTER LOADING AN A-6 INTRUDER.

FOLLOWING PAGE, THE COMBAT DIRECTION CENTER (CDC) OF THE *GEORGE WASHINGTON* RESPONDS TO CONTACT AND INTELLIGENCE INFORMATION BY DIRECTING THE ACTIONS OF THE SHIP'S AIR ASSETS.

ABOVE, FIRE CONTROLMEN EXERCISE AT
DETECTING AN INCOMING MISSILE AND FIR-
ING A DEFENSIVE SEA SPARROW MISSILE TO
"PROTECT" THE USS *GEORGE WASHINGTON.*

TECHNICIANS CHECK OUT THE OPERATION OF
THE CLOSE-IN WEAPONS SYSTEM (CIWS), THE
CLOSE-RANGE DEFENSE AGAINST LOW- AND
FAST-FLYING MISSILES OR AIRCRAFT.

CDC AND ITS WATCH STANDERS ON BOARD

THE *KITTY HAWK*.

in sync—having the same "picture" to be able to counter any potential threats. The air-warfare module works through air-intercept controllers, the guys "out front" in those E-2C planes with the "Frisbee" radar domes, to direct all of our aircraft in intercepting inbound "raids" or to identify potential hostiles.

The display and most of the dissemination functions of CDC take place here in the display and decision (D&D) module, where all of the information collected in the other modules is focused for the TAO. These two large—forty-six-inch—screen displays use symbols and a slew of status boards, which give key tactical information. Here, the TAO controls the ship's self-defense weapons—the Close-in Weapons System (CIWS), the NATO Sea Sparrow Missile System, as well as the air wing aircraft. The TAO gets his guidance for the use of these through the Captain's battle orders and in the absence of the Captain has weapons-release authority for the defense of the ship. When ordered by the TAO to engage an air target, the ship's weapons coordinator prioritizes engagements and sends verbal and electronic orders to the appropriate defensive operators. For surface and submarine engagements, he directs the respective watch officer to carry out the engagement. When we're in a strike role, rather than defensive, D&D also checks all launching aircraft for valid IFF codes and gives them initial vectors to their targets.

One thing that should be apparent by just looking at the screens and the numbers of contacts today—in peacetime—is that the situation can rapidly get so saturated that the time for decision and action may be seconds, or even less!

OK—the carrier has its radars, and they're very effective for air threats within their radar horizon, which is dependent on two fixed heights or altitudes: first, the height of the radar; second, the altitude of the threat aircraft. The horizon in miles is 1.14 times the square root of the height of eye (or radar)—for example, an aircraft flying at 40,000 feet can cover the ocean with radar out to a radius of over 200 miles, while the ship's radar can reach targets on the surface, or a plane or missile flying "on the deck," only out to—say—at best a couple of tens of miles, dependent on threat altitude. Getting the radar up high is the way to go, obviously. That's where we come in—the good old slow Grumman Hawkeye. Look at us as an adjunct of the ship—its sensor stuck out ahead, picking up surface targets the ship can't pick up, as well as aircraft or missiles high and low. Plus, we have the picture of our own guys for the Combat Direction Center. We're the only way you can pick up a supersonic threat and direct our fighters to it far enough out to keep its missiles from getting to the ship. We like to think we keep the admiral out of trouble!

Look at our capability. Besides that powerful radar that looks like a big Frisbee, we have IFF [Identification Friend or Foe] and passive detectors. The frequency of the radar gives us far better capability than the ship's radars—we can even beat some threats people don't think we can, like certain "stealth" measures. So with its range when we're at altitude, and coupled with the fact we're always moving—sweeping— we cover millions of square miles. All our sensors feed into a general-purpose computer, so we can handle warning, threat analysis, and countermeasures against aircraft, missile, or surface targets. We can maintain over six hundred tracks and are capable, for instance, of tracking all the humongous air traffic from Boston to Washington when we're over New York! We have three controllers in the back end of the aircraft, and with five radios we're busy as a one-armed paperhanger with hands and even our feet tracking, designating, and communicating to the ship and aircraft we're directing to targets.

Slower than the jets, yeah, but we're up for the long ride—good endurance! We might just be the most important airplane in the air wing! I'm convinced!

AIR CONTROLLER

We're in the Carrier Air Traffic Control Center, or CATCC. As you can see, the Navy has made a major investment in air controllers, technicians, and traffic-control equipment. These aren't the old days of the old movies, where the LSO with his flags waved a Hellcat or a dive-bomber—an SBD—onto the flight deck. With these jets and the

OPPOSITE, ELECTRONIC TECHNICIANS MAKE FINE ADJUSTMENTS TO RADAR HIGH UP ON THE ISLAND OF THE CARRIER.

amount of traffic we see, it takes a lot of help to get them aboard in all-weather conditions.

We've got two work centers here, Air Operations and Carrier-Controlled Approach, and between them we get safe, orderly, and expeditious control of aircraft to and from the carrier. Air Ops puts out the daily air plan and acts as a clearinghouse for all events. You see status boards showing frequencies, aircraft numbers, pilots, mission, "divert fields"—where to send a plane if it runs low on fuel or has another problem—things like that. The air ops officer uses this data to help recommend best courses of action in an emergency.

Carrier-Controlled Approach is a control room where aircraft are given separation [distance between aircraft] and positive radar control during bad weather and at night. It's probably the last bastion of true "seat of the pants" air-traffic control. Controllers must be able to respond on a moment's notice. We're always expediting the launch and recovery of aircraft to minimize the time the carrier has to head into the wind. Sometimes that permits only a short run. We put the planes about twenty miles from the boat on a bearing as close as possible to the final landing course. As they enter "holding," we give them an

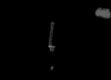

expected time to begin their approaches, normally a minute apart, all based on the relative position of the holding "stack" to our course and the "ready deck" time predicted by the air boss. As they start their approach, they are handed off to one of two approach controllers, who ensures that each plane on his frequency keeps enough separation from the other aircraft, and he gives vectors for each plane to fly. The whole job is very similar to what civilian controllers do at busy airports, with two exceptions—they don't have many waveoffs from moving decks or failures to catch a wire, and we don't have their pay! Most of us wouldn't want to give up our job, though—there's something about this life that's contagious!

Hair-raising experiences? Well, after fifteen years of controlling, six at sea, there've been a lot, though the hair may be getting to where it won't raise. The most tense for me was one night when I was controlling tankers. An A-6 made one poor pass at the deck and reported very low fuel state on turning downwind. I had to position the overhead tanker to provide fuel if he missed again. I set up the tanker to be ahead of the A-6 as he touched down, but the tanker was late descending from altitude. The A-6 bolted, went to power, and looked for his tanker—now behind him, but slower. Both raced ahead, the A-6 winning the race and moving out. I quickly put the A-6 in a slow left turn and told the tanker what was up. The A-6 caught on, and he slowed down; meanwhile, the tanker put the pedal down to catch up. As both completed their turns back toward the ship, the tanker was now too far ahead of the A-6, and neither could see the other because of clouds. "Sweat Condition One" was under way in CATCC! The ship started rigging the barricade in case they couldn't get joined [the barricade is a net that stretches across the landing area to catch a plane that's damaged or, in this case, that might not have enough fuel to try again in case of a bolter; barricade landings are called "controlled crashes"]. A second tanker checked in with me at this point, so I vectored him to a spot above the two planes. The first two then joined up—but the A-6 wasn't getting any fuel through the hose! Only a few minutes from possible flameout [running out of fuel]! I climbed the A-6 again, hooked him up to the second tanker—and he got fuel. On reconstructing, I found the second tanker hadn't been scheduled for our event—but thank God! They say they don't want you if you're not lucky!

QUARTERMASTER

We get the ship where it needs to go—us and the navigator. In the old days most navigation was by celestial means, that is, shooting the altitude of a well-known star or planet with a sextant and solving a geometry problem, plotting where the lines of position crossed. You will still see officers and quartermasters getting practice with the sex-

A QUARTERMASTER IN THE *KITTY HAWK* FIXES THE SHIP'S POSITION ON A CHART DURING ITS DEPARTURE FROM THE SAN DIEGO SHIP CHANNEL.

PREVIOUS PAGE, IN THE *GEORGE WASHINGTON'S* CARRIER AIR TRAFFIC CONTROL CENTER (CATCC), THE ACTIVITY OFTEN RESEMBLES THAT OF A BEEHIVE AS AIR CONTROLLERS CONTROL MULTIPLE AIRCRAFT MUCH IN THE MANNER OF THEIR CIVILIAN COUNTERPARTS AT THE BUSIER COMMERCIAL HUBS.

tant, but total reliability on the stars is a thing of the past. I do it a lot because it's a big part of my exams for advancement, and you forget how to use the navigation tables and almanacs if you don't use them.

Keeping the charts up to date takes up a lot of time. Every time a navigation aid is changed, we get a notice and have to correct the charts. It's important: if we plot them wrong, we could run aground, and captains who do that aren't happy campers!

The new gadgets are fantastic, even if they might cost us our job some day. With GPS [the Global Positioning System] we can tell where we are within thirty feet anywhere in the world, and all we have to do is take a few seconds to push a few buttons and the satellites do the rest. Of course, electronics and computers can fail, so quartermasters have to keep up on how to use all the aids, radio direction finding, Loran, using the Fathometer to navigate by sounding lines, and pilot-ing—you know, taking and plotting bearings to lighthouses, beacons, and landmarks—and recommending safe courses to the officer of the deck. We're one of the few ratings that haven't changed too much with the modern electronic world. Us, the signalmen, and boatswain's mates are about the last of the "Old Navy"—the real sailors!

I think the trickiest time for the navigator is when coming in or out of port. The currents and winds play more in setting the ship off the safe course, and then there's always the sightseers who run sailboats or power boats right under the bow where we can't see them. Suicidal maniacs! If they only knew that it takes this ship about two miles to come to a stop from full speed—man! But coming in or out of port is fun; there's lots to see, and it's an adventure to visit foreign ports. Didn't we join the Navy to see the world?

SIGNALMAN

Our job is to take care of the signal flags and to communicate with other ships by semaphore or blinker—that's the Morse code. One nice thing about being a signalman is that you get a good seat for whatever goes on down on the flight deck or in the miles of ocean around us. Lots of fresh air and sunshine—sometimes too much! The main thing we have to do is hoist signal flags in International Code to tell other ships what we're doing—like conducting flight ops, when we have to maintain a course into the wind, and so we really aren't free to take avoiding courses. It's the "Old Navy" really. Today you have so many radio circuits and can send messages on UHF or VHF, all that stuff, so a lot of people think we don't really need signalmen any more. But when we have to go to radio silence—EMCON [emission control]—the blinker or the flags are what we use. Also, that's mostly what we use when we operate with other countries, like during NATO exercises.

Right now, during this UNREP, we're sending semaphore to the

BELOW, **DESPITE THE ENCROACHING TECH-NOLOGY THAT DOOMS TO OBSOLESCENCE MANY OF THE TECHNIQUES USED BY SAILORS IN THE PAST, QUARTERMASTERS MAINTAIN PROFICIENCY WITH THE SEXTANT, HERE "SHOOTING THE SUN."**

ABOVE, SIGNALMEN OF THE MODERN NAVY REMAIN BUSY WITH
SIGNALS TRANSMITTED BY TRADITIONAL SIGNAL FLAGS.

A KITTY HAWK SIGNALMAN SILHOUETTED AGAINST THE SUNSET
DURING FLIGHT OPERATIONS IN THE PACIFIC OCEAN.

tanker, telling the details of the fuel transfer. That signalman is pretty good. See how he hardly comes to a stop with his arms with each letter he sends? Our man is a hot shot—he holds his flags so it tells them when he's got the word he's sending, but he's rubbing it in a little—just a little "dis": he keeps his flags out the whole time the tanker guy sends, meaning, "Go ahead, give me your best, fastest shot, I've got you 100 percent."

No, that signalman sending with his arms and no flags isn't on watch. He's goofing off. See that marine with him? Well, that's a signal*woman* he's sending to over there—see her answering? He's setting up a date for the marine with the woman, and they're having a lot of laughs back and forth with where they'll meet in Norfolk when we're in port—keeping a little fun in the program!

The Navy's a pretty good life, but I'll probably leave when this hitch is up. I really have trouble seeing what my training as a signalman would set me up for after a twenty-year career; of course, I picked it several years ago! I also don't go so much for this "big ship" stuff. I really liked being on a frigate—you know the whole crew, and you get closer to buddies. Here you can drown in people—just take a look at the chow lines! But most of the crew seems to like it, and the crew does one hell of a job! We earn our pay!

RADIOMAN

This is a busy, busy place! But can you imagine what a radio room today would look like if we were back in the "good old days" of using headsets, HF [high frequency], a manual key, and an operator with earphones sending out, "Da dit, dit dit da, dit dit dit" at twenty-five words a minute? With the number of channels we have today, all of the equipment, we'd have to have a separate ship to carry all those radiomen! It looks complex, doesn't it? But count the radiomen—very few. That's automation and digital processing. Want to try something? Ask how many radiomen in our gang can copy Morse—would you bet three? Two? How about *one?* Those old days are gone in this Navy.

Twenty years ago nobody would have listened to you if you said that some day the radio field and the computer field would merge to be one and the same. It's here! Unfortunately, because we have the capability, we've lost one of the basics of communication: brevity! Today we don't know how to say anything in a few words; because we can transmit and handle the *Wall Street Journal* in a few micro-bursts of energy, we *do* it. There's so much information available that I think our bosses must just about drown in it. But we do the job. Somehow the load keeps growing, and somehow it gets processed. It seems to me that the main increases aren't in the tactical ship and airplane things—it seems that the monstrous loads are in intelligence traffic.

ABOVE, A RADIOMAN CHECKS OUT COMMU-

NICATIONS EQUIPMENT IN THE RADIO ROOM

OF THE *KITTY HAWK.*

A *GEORGE WASHINGTON* SIGNALMAN

RECEIVES A SEMAPHORE MESSAGE FROM

THE NUCLEAR CRUISER *BAINBRIDGE.*

AEROGRAPHER'S MATE, WEATHER LEADING PETTY OFFICER

"Weather guessing" has come a long way in the last twenty or thirty years. Satellites and digital signal processing are here today, and we have the ability to look at the weather situation for thousands of miles instead of just at the visual horizon. We still use the old-style maps to plot cold fronts and warm fronts, but transmission of facsimile, which was one of our first real breakthroughs, means that we are really up to the minute with changes. Now with this latest equipment we can see the Pacific coastline of the United States, our operating areas overlaid, and then the feed from satellites showing the weather. We can blow up the picture and get a snapshot of even local weather. Just a few minutes ago, the Captain asked us what course he should take to get to a fairly clear area in about an hour. We have a training squadron coming in to give student pilots their first carrier landings, and we hope to avoid having them fight all of this slop we have here. It's hard enough the first time in sparkling bluebird weather! We picked out an area that looks better, and the Captain's steaming over there. See, he trusts us—or our modern systems.

We send up weather balloons with transmitting sensors to help fill in the information needed on upper-altitude winds and temperatures, those sorts of things. We give weather briefs and have the info for the air wing whenever they need it, and one of us goes up to the bridge with charts to brief the Captain before the start of flight ops. Weather's really important for any military operation, but a carrier is really a "star" user.

BELOW-DECKS FUELS CHIEF

OK—my crew below-decks takes care of storing and pumping JP-5 [jet fuel] for the aircraft. Down on the seventh deck we coordinate moving fuel between fifteen flight-deck and five hangar-deck stations, two pump rooms, and the tanks. We assure the quality of the JP-5 and take care of the pumps, filters, purifiers, tanks, and lube-oil systems. Pure JP-5 is our major concern. When we defuel aircraft, we let that contaminated fuel settle out in special tanks. Then we run it through centrifugal purifiers to a service tank. Our filters will screen out even tiny impurities, as small as five microns—a hair from your head is one hundred microns. We take thousands of samples a month, doing water and sediment as well as flash-point checks. The pump room is a tough place to get to, but it's pretty—with all the pipes painted purple. The pump-room operator is an important watch, operating and maintaining JP-5 pumps, filters, and purifiers.

OPPOSITE, AEROGRAPHER'S MATES RELEASE A WEATHER BALLOON WITH A TELEMETRY TRANSMITTER FROM THE STERN OF THE USS *GEORGE WASHINGTON.*

FOLLOWING PAGE, IN THE PUMP ROOM, DEEP WITHIN THE *GEORGE WASHINGTON,* AN AVIATION-FUELS SPECIALIST TRANSFERS JET FUEL, USING HAND SIGNALS TO COMMUNICATE PUMP ACTIONS.

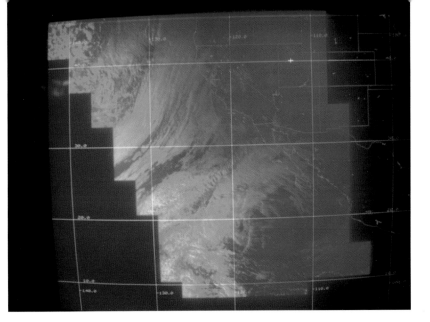

RIGHT, TODAY'S AEROGRAPHER'S MATES PREDICT WEATHER WITH THE ASSISTANCE OF SATELLITES AND HIGH-TECH SIGNAL-PROCESSING EQUIPMENT THAT PROVIDE A REAL-TIME PICTURE OF CLOUD COVERAGE SUPERIMPOSED, AS HERE, OVER AN OUTLINE OF THE AREA OFF SAN DIEGO.

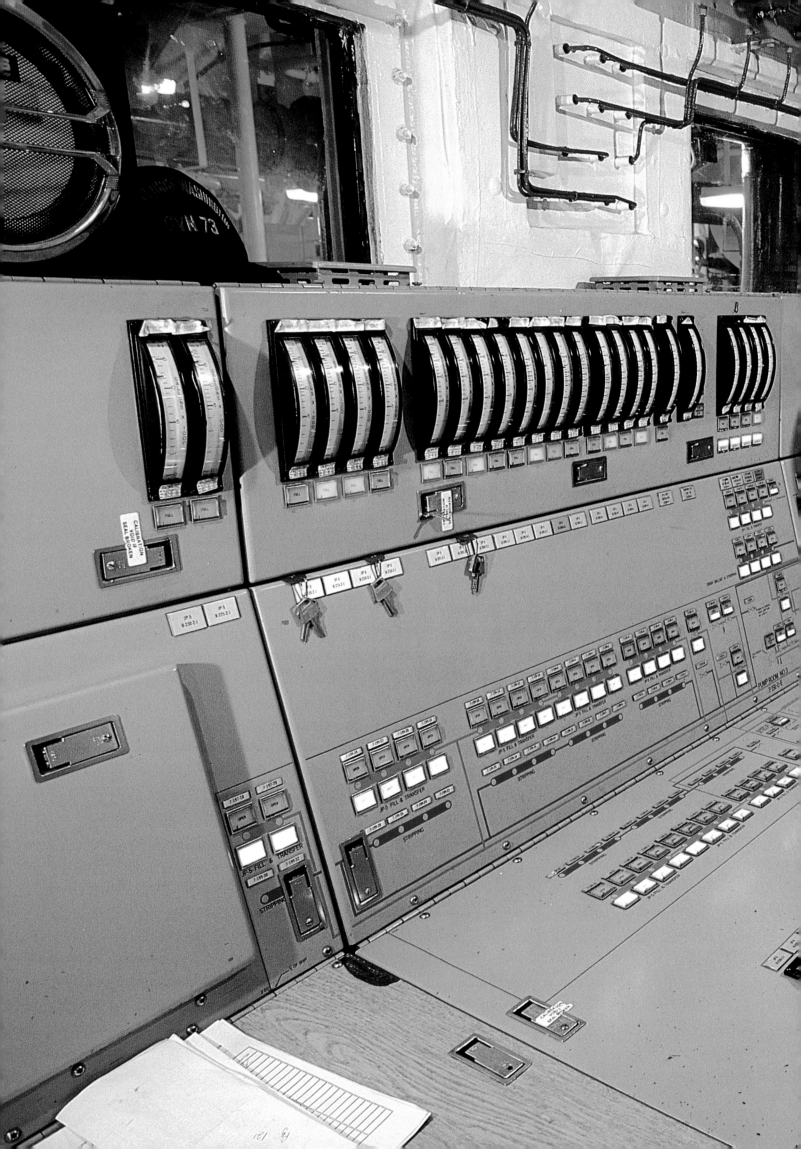

ENGINE ROOM WATCH

There's lots of things that a big ship like this can do—launch and land airplanes, drop bombs, shoot down other planes, show the flag, win battles, keep from having wars—and everyone on board feels that the job he does is the most important. Fact is, none of them can do *anything—not a single damned thing*—if the ship can't get there, wherever "there" is! You don't hear as much about us, but *we* get you there—the engineers! If we don't do our job, this whole thing is just a sitting duck—one big floating island—and all it can shoot is Sea Sparrows (and that's "maybe") or the marines' small arms!

In an engineering watch section we have a lot of different types working. First off, we have the engineering officer of the watch who oversees everything that we do. On a football team, he'd be the quarterback. He makes sure that we do everything by the book, that we properly answer the "bells" signaled by the officer of the deck on the bridge, that the throttleman opens steam from the turbines so that the propellers go ahead or back as ordered and not the wrong way! Then we have the offensive line—the workers, the machinists' mates like me, the ones who get dirty and greasy. We're the heart and soul of the ship! We operate the steam plant, condensers, lube-oil systems. We test lube oil; run the distilling plants that make our drinking water; take action to correct out-of-spec alarms, like salinity or lube-oil pressure or temperature alarms; fix steam and oil leaks; and generally do the things in maintenance to make sure the engineering plant can make us go for six months away from home. There's lots of hours of logging gauge and meter readings, too—that's boring!

On fossil-fuel plants like the *Saratoga* or *Kennedy,* we would light off the boilers, just like the old days—light an oily rag torch, stick it in the firebox, and hope it doesn't blow up. On the nukes, it's much neater and sophisticated. They have like a kicker in football, the specialist: a reactor operator, an RO, brings the plant "critical," like turning up an electric stove. In the fossil plants we have BTs—boiler tenders—who really are like chemists because they measure the amounts of various chemicals added to the boiler water to prevent corrosion. On the

ENGINEERING WATCH STANDERS IN CENTRAL CONTROL DURING NORMAL STEAMING, ON BOARD THE *KITTY HAWK* IN THE PACIFIC.

ABOVE, IN THE CONVENTIONAL-PROPULSION POWER PLANT OF THE USS *SARATOGA*, ENGINEERING WATCH STANDERS LIGHT OFF THE OIL-FIRED BOILER.

OPPOSITE, *TOP*, AN ENGINE-ROOM WATCH STANDER MONITORS THE EQUIPMENT AND LOGS ITS PERFORMANCE PARAMETERS IN THE *KITTY HAWK*.

RIGHT, A PROPELLER SHAFT, ONE OF FOUR THAT DRIVE THE SHIP, PASSES THROUGH THE HULL FAR DOWN IN THE STERN OF THE *SARATOGA*.

ABOVE, AN ARRAY OF LUBRICATING-OIL
SAMPLES DRAWN FOR TESTING TO ENSURE
THE HIGH QUALITY OF VITAL LUBRICANTS
FOR THE ENGINEERING MACHINERY OF THE
SARATOGA.

AN ELECTRICAL-PANEL WATCH STANDER IN
THE ENGINE ROOM FINDS THE ROUTINE LESS
THAN ACTIVE IN NORMAL SITUATIONS, BUT IT
CAN BE ENERGIZED TO A BEDLAM LEVEL
WHEN SYSTEMS MALFUNCTION.

nukes, they don't have BTs; they use those good old MMs—machinists' mates—and make them specialists called ELTs, engineering-lab technicians, who do all the chemistry in the secondary plant—the steam plant—as well as monitoring, measuring, and correcting the reactor-plant chemistry. These guys are also the experts in monitoring radiation and in carrying out radioactive controls. Really, they are some of the smartest men on the ship—maybe just under the ROs, who are great electronic technicians even if they do get razzed a lot.

The electricians are a lot like machinists' mates. They work hard, keep a lot of motors and generators humming, troubleshoot, hunt for "grounds" in thousands of miles of wiring and cables, and stand a lot of boring watches keeping logs and monitoring frequencies to correct a situation if something malfunctions. But those guys standing those "routine" watches are worth their weight in gold when a pipe or valve springs a leak or when a fire starts! That's when every cent you spend on an engineer on watch pays off!

REACTOR OPERATOR

I guess I'm a little different. I'm a reactor operator, but I'm also a second-generation "nuke"! My dad was a nuke before I was born and trained in nuclear prototypes in the desert in Idaho, same as I did, only he says he wouldn't be a "prima donna RO"—reactor operator. I tell him that he probably wasn't smart enough; we razz each other a lot. But you know, a lot of people think of nuclear power as something that just happened yesterday; they don't focus on the fact that the first nuclear ship went to sea over thirty years ago! He has lots of sea stories about the old days, how tough the nuclear schools and training were then, and how at the start the nukes were really kind of an elite corps, and how so many of the enlisted guys made officer and a lot of the officers he worked for made admiral. Some of the funniest stories are about the way that old Admiral Rickover stirred people up in the shipyards and at the prototypes: when he came to visit, the top brass didn't have enough panic buttons to push!

Well, I tell my dad that I have news for him—the nuke training is tougher today than when he was in. Way tougher! The people at the training places know more things to ask, and they've been at this "safety" stuff longer than most people have in careers. I counted them one time—almost two hundred submarine reactors at sea, twenty-two carrier plants (eight on the *Enterprise* alone!), and fifteen or twenty nuke cruiser reactors—all those and zero accidents! The training and good people pay off! Not to mention the care and tough standards in building them. The differences between my dad's day and now are, one, it's tougher and more rigid, more spelled out in tight procedures, and two, the "mystique" of being in a small, hand-picked group has

A THROTTLEMAN RESPONDS TO SPEED ORDERS TRANSMITTED FROM THE BRIDGE, OPENING A VALVE TO PASS MORE STEAM TO THE TURBINES TO INCREASE THE SHIP'S SPEED.

gone away pretty much—there's lots of us. The only "mystique" is that the power plants are classified for security—only "cleared" people can get access to the manuals or the plants.

By basic and advanced training I am really an electronics technician, but after that training I was selected for nuclear training. Six months of very tough academic training and then six more of practical operational training got me to my first nuclear ship, where I spent months of fourteen- to sixteen-hour days learning my job and qualifying on the nuclear plant. It isn't enough just to know your own job—you have to be very, very familiar with every other watch station, since any one of them can have an impact on the overall plant safety. We require each and every man to be able to understand and to explain how every action he takes impacts upon the reactor, reactivity, safety, and radiation. All of these things are closely interrelated, and all engineering personnel must understand just how they influence the plant.

My job is to operate the controls that determine the amount of heat we get from nuclear fission to produce steam for our turbines and electrical generators. The heat that makes steam in the steam generators is basically the same heat that oil-fired boilers produce in fossil-fuel plants. Once you get steam, the plants are about identical in components, piping, etc. Yes, there is radiation, but the construction of the plant and careful, safe operation by people who fully understand the potential impact of each and every operation they perform makes concern about nuclear radiation a minor concern. A person in a year on board an operating nuclear ship receives far less radiation than you get from cosmic radiation—way, way less than if you live in "mile high" Denver! Because of our shielding and rigid specifications on the doses we allow, radiation from an operating reactor plant is of little concern, but that doesn't mean we aren't checking it everywhere on a daily basis. They teach us down here in the engineering spaces that "complacency is the enemy!"

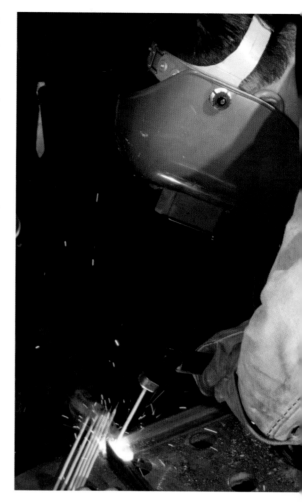

HIGHLY QUALIFIED WELDERS ON BOARD CARRIERS PROVIDE A REPAIR CAPABILITY EXTENDING TO THE DEMANDING LEVEL OF NUCLEAR-PLANT REPAIR.

MAINTENANCE OFFICER

Most people think of an aircraft carrier in terms of most other surface ships, that is, that they have tenders or bases to do all their maintenance work. Not so! We're a very self-sufficient ship, with virtually all of the capabilities that a destroyer tender or a submarine tender has as far as shops go. We have a superb carpenter shop, capable of doing just about anything with wood that can be done anywhere in the Navy. Our machine shops are very complete. What do you need? Our sailors can turn out pieces on the lathe; they can cut very intricate gears, with straight teeth or helical; they can produce threaded bolts as accurately as anyone else; and they can cut or grind pieces to replace original installations. We have welders who can perform as well as welders any-

ABOVE, THE MACHINE SHOPS IN THE USS
GEORGE WASHINGTON GIVE THE CARRIER
A TREMENDOUS CAPABILITY FOR THE
REPAIR AND MAINTENANCE OF EQUIP-
MENT. HERE, A PETTY OFFICER MANU-
FACTURES A CLOSE-TOLERANCE REPAIR
PART.

LIQUID OXYGEN OF THE HIGHEST QUALITY
IS SEPARATED FROM NITROGEN IN THE
AIR BY EQUIPMENT IN THE GEORGE
WASHINGTON AND TRANSFERRED TO
HIGH-PRESSURE STORAGE BOTTLES AND
TANKS.

where, including highly trained and qualified stainless-steel welders who can tackle difficult repair or maintenance on our nuclear power plant. Our electrical shops can rewire motors or repair electrical breakers or switches. We produce liquid oxygen with our oxygen generator in still another shop, and I think you'll be interested in watching our men transfer some into a pressurized canister—it comes out a beautiful aquamarine blue, if you can see through the heavy fog of gaseous oxygen!

As we speak, our engraving-machine operator is starting to cut a special job for you, incidentally.

When we deploy with a battle group, most of the ships look at us as a source of repair for their sick equipment, and we're happy to help—it's all one Navy, isn't it? Besides, we enjoy the challenge of producing a part that some other crew thinks is impossible to get. One thing that's our pride and joy is our cal lab, the calibration lab—it specializes in "the science of measurement": they fix, calibrate, or adjust precise gauges, thermometers, clocks, electrical instruments, and just about any instrument found in ships. From our lab we send specialized teams to ships of the battle group to help them with their calibration loads. Our guys pack up several hundred pounds of gear and transfer over to another ship to do their job, bringing the instruments up to within the accuracy standards acceptable to the National Bureau of Standards. Early in deployment they did five hundred gauges in one day!

I've been in the Navy twenty-two years, enlisted and officer, and I really like the kind of self-sufficiency we have in carriers. This is my second carrier, and I hope to stay in them.

Here's your very special, personalized name tag our guys made for you as we talked! Fast, huh? All in a day's work!

DAMAGE CONTROLMAN

You're here in damage-control central at a good time—GQ [general quarters: when the entire crew man their battle stations]. You can get a good picture of what we do when we simulate a battle situation. This is the time when our rating, damage controlman [DC], pays off for the ship. We're the specialists at fixing leaking or burst piping, blown gaskets, or holes in the hull from bombs or shells: our job is keeping the ship afloat and fighting. We study all of the ship's systems and construction so that we're experts on them. We have "flying squads" organized and located in a number of places, so when a pipe bursts or starts spewing out oil or water, or if you have a fire, the announcement on the MC system or on the phones gets the nearest damage controlman running to the scene with damage-control equipment. We don't train only the DCs: just about everyone in the crew has some training in some sort of damage control.

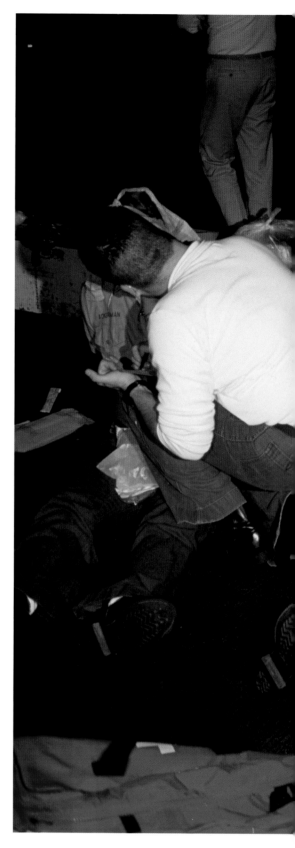

A MASS-CASUALTY DRILL ON THE HANGAR DECK OF THE USS *KITTY HAWK* GIVES THE CREW PRACTICE IN HANDLING DAMAGE-CONTROL AND FIRE-FIGHTING EQUIPMENT UNDER A WORST-CASE SCENARIO, WHEN GRAVE WOUNDS ABOUND AND TRIAGE IS NECESSARY.

In here, we have guys from different departments, experts at knowing their spaces, and they keep damage or unusual situations plotted on those detailed ship plans that you see them pulling out from the bulkheads. Those are classified "confidential" because of the detail. You can find every space on the ship—thousands—on those plan views and side views. See, they have lights showing whether a valve is open or shut. We can order a space to be flooded to balance the ship—if a compartment on the port side is flooded, we can balance it by flooding one on the starboard side.

Some damage is simple—it might be controlled by wrapping a small pipe with marline and tying it off; others will take plastic patching, some will take plugs driven in with heavy hammers. Some spaces will require the bulkheads to be shored up—that's what those long wood four-by-fours you see along some of the passageways are for.

We train sailors to perform with protective gear—breathing masks and stuff. They can even work underwater in a flooded space. It's a real challenge trying to put a patch on a burst pipe against high water pressure!

OK—they've just announced a plane attacking with a torpedo. See, everyone is leaning against the desk or a bulkhead, feet apart, knees flexed, to offset the shock of the hit. We do lots of drills on this—same

ARTIFICIAL SMOKE GENERATORS PROVIDE REALISM TO A FIRE DRILL IN AN ISOLATED COMPARTMENT OF THE *GEORGE WASHINGTON.*

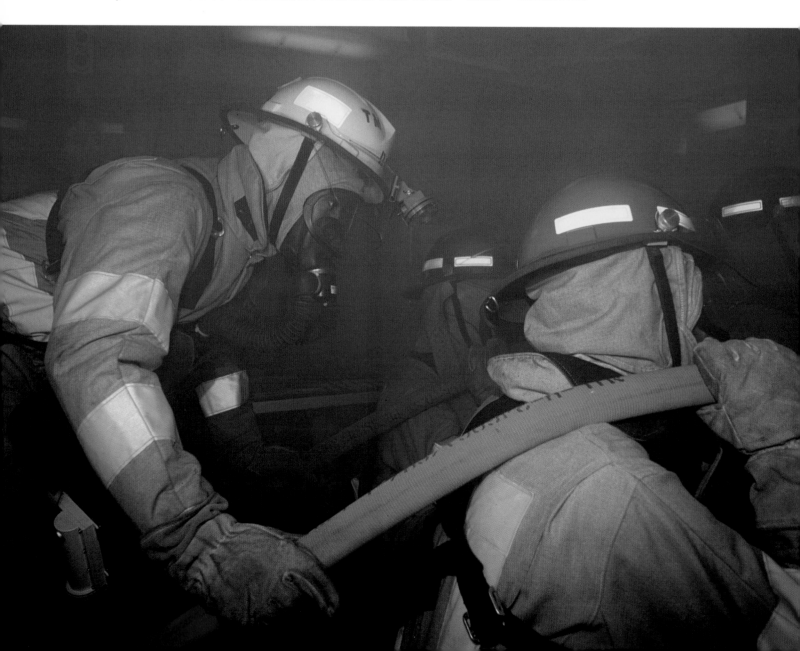

with fire-fighting—we do it on board and in special training places on the beach.

I've heard that the modern carriers are really unsinkable, that even if all the compartments are flooded, there's enough positive buoyancy built into the sponsons to keep it afloat, but I wouldn't take a chance. Hard to believe when you look at the old movies of damage and fires in war! An out-of-control fire on the hangar deck? A nightmare!

ELECTRONICS REPAIR TECHNICIAN

We like to feel that there's no job in the field of microminiaturized circuitry that's beyond us—but we really aren't there yet! We can do a lot of things that a few years ago I wouldn't have believed would come to pass. We have several sections of our electronics shops in the Aircraft Intermediate Maintenance Division [AIMD], which do different things. Some calibrate avionics instrumentation, and it can involve a lot of physical, mechanical things. We can test modules with what you will see is pretty complex and sophisticated test equipment, which spits out "go" or "no go" as we march through the itemized steps. Then, you can see some of us in this shop working with very fine stuff—printed circuitry and multichannel solid-state equipment—and it's so fine that we have to use microscopes to see our work. It's no place for a man with the shakes! Very delicate work—with a lot of special tools, many of which look just like dental tools, and probably were. It's a capability that's really added to our carrier's ability to be self-sustaining and independent—not as much tied to the apron strings of the supply system.

ENGINE SHOP LEADING PETTY OFFICER

Jet engines are pretty rugged and can take an amazing amount of punishment when you consider the close tolerances of the turbine blading. Take a look at that A-6 engine that was FOD'ed. A steel bolt was picked up in the intake, passed through the blading, and really only nicked several blades badly! Of course, we changed the engine, but if that pilot had been in a battle situation and that FOD had been due to hostile fire, he'd have made it back, no sweat.

Here in the jet shop we do engine work that's beyond what the squadron level of maintenance is able to do. If it's a bigger job than we can handle, we fly that engine back on a COD flight to be worked on ashore—we call that "depot maintenance." A lot of people are amazed that one of these powerful and complex jet engines can be changed out on board. That's just one of the many tough jobs that our AIMD people take on. Much of our work takes a lot of hours, and it's very tedious. In many cases, we have to lean on the Supply Department to get us specialized parts, and once we have those in hand, we start

A *KITTY HAWK* FIREFIGHTER PREPARES TO ENTER THE "FLAMING" COMPARTMENT.

reassembling the engine, check out every nut and bolt, and give it a check run in the test cell out there on the stern outside the hangar deck.

Right now we have a helicopter engine in the cell, so you can see—and especially hear—the test run. We run the engine at specific speeds, and the diagnostic equipment records the parameters that show us the performance of the engine after repair. Meeting each parameter is mandatory—we're talking about lives at stake, lives of the pilots and lives of the crews. There's no "almost" or "halfway"—the green light only goes off for a 100-percent job.

PHOTOGRAPHER'S MATE

This is really a "state of the art" photo lab! That machine you see over there is a "first" in the fleet. We can digitize photographs and manipulate them fantastically if we want. It's not just a simple thing like taking pictures and printing them that counts—we can have a photo taken, process it, transmit it, and have it in the hands of a news-paper or TV studio in minutes or hours: really up-to-the-minute. Just think what this can do for a commander in the field as far as intelli-

OPPOSITE, A CARRIER'S JET-ENGINE SHOPS ARE CAPABLE OF REPAIRING DAMAGED TURBINE BLADING, REPLACING ENGINES, AND TESTING ENGINES ON SPECIALIZED EQUIPMENT PRIOR TO INSTALLATION. HIGHLY SKILLED TECHNICIANS IN THE *KITTY HAWK* REPLACE BLADES DAMAGED WHEN THIS ENGINE INGESTED A BOLT.

LEFT, A PETTY OFFICER IN THE *GEORGE WASHINGTON* PREPARES TV ENTERTAINMENT PROGRAMS FOR THE CREW'S VIEWING.

BELOW, A PHOTOGRAPHER'S MATE IN THE STATE-OF-THE-ART LABORATORY OF THE *GEORGE WASHINGTON* DIGITALLY MANIPU-LATES THE IMAGE OF AN F/A-18 HORNET AND HIS SHIP IN A PHOTOGRAPH FOUND EARLIER IN THIS BOOK (SEE PAGE 22).

gence goes. The big load most of the time is for PR—public relations. Every VIP who visits gets photographs to take home, to show people back in some little town in Iowa just what their taxes pay for. They can see carrier sailors working around-the-clock and around the world. Our bosses in the Pentagon and fleet staffs hit us hard all the time for good action photos, so we have photographers shooting from helos and out on the flight deck daily. How busy is our processing lab? Well, on our six-month deployment, which was a busy one PR-wise, we processed more than forty-five thousand color photos and over twenty-one thousand prints on our color copier!

Here's a sample of modern technology you should appreciate. This VIP guest with the Captain up on the bridge was wearing a baseball cap advertising farm machinery—not our ship cap, as you can see. In a couple of hours we manipulated the image to this—see, he's now wearing our ship cap, with all the gold braid! Look again—we took off that grease spot on his jacket! On another photo we gave the admiral a full head of hair! Who says photos don't lie?

SUPPLY OFFICER

A job in Supply in an aircraft carrier is about the most challenging job I can imagine. Let me tell you, there're challenges every single day—things that seem hard to do or too hard to even consider—and boredom is not one of my problems! It would take us a full day to visit all of the Supply Department spaces—dozens of storerooms for food and supplies, all of the cooking and eating spaces, computer and records spaces—boy!

First off, there's the normal kind of thing you think of—spare parts. We carry tens of thousands of them, just the "line items," and for some individual items we might have thousands on board in our supply bins. Everything is highly computerized, so we know exactly where it is and how many we have, and we reorder at a certain stock level—that sort of thing. We get super service from our Navy supply depots and aviation depots, and with our ability to fly items out on COD planes we seldom have much in the way of delays because of equipment outages.

But let's go beyond this. We're the department that our sailors look to for chow—twenty thousand individual meals served a day in our mess halls and wardrooms, plus gosh-knows how many box lunches during flight ops. And coffee—don't forget Navy coffee, although these days a lot of the youngsters have a preference for the soft drinks that we also provide. Think about the gross numbers: in a day, three hundred to four hundred dozen eggs, five hundred to six hundred gallons of milk! Our mess-management specialists—what we used to call cooks, bakers, stewards, and mess cooks—work around-the-clock. A tired sailor can get something to eat at any hour of the day or night.

ONE OF THE MANY FUNCTIONS OF A VERY BUSY AND VITAL SUPPLY DEPARTMENT, THE LAUNDRY MUST RESPOND TO THE CLEANING AND PRESSING NEEDS OF A SMALL-CITY-SIZED CREW. THE CREW'S LAUNDRY IS BAGGED AND HANDLED BY DIVISIONS IN A ONE-DAY TURNAROUND.

THE *KITTY HAWK* BARBERS AND "CUSTOMERS" FIND AMUSING THIS MARINE'S INSISTENCE ON THE CUT THAT IS THE TRADEMARK OF THE CORPS.

OPPOSITE, THE "PAY LINE" OF PAST SAILORS' MEMO-
RIES IS GONE! HERE IN THE *KITTY HAWK*, THE DISBURS-
ING OFFICER BREAKS A SWEAT AT THE RESPONSIBILITY
OF TAKING ONE MILLION DOLLARS FROM HIS SAFE
FOR TRANSPORT TO AND LOADING INTO THE AUTO-
MATIC TELLER MACHINES THAT NOW SERVE AS PAY-
MASTER. *RIGHT,* VIDEO GAMES ON THE MESS DECKS
OF THE *GEORGE WASHINGTON* ARE VERY POPULAR,
OFTEN DRAWING A WAITING LINE EAGER TO INSERT
QUARTERS, MANY OF WHICH END UP FINANCING
TOURS AND ENTERTAINMENT ACTIVITIES. *BELOW,*
MANY LARGE STOREROOMS HOLD PROVISIONS AND
REPAIR PARTS THAT ENABLE CARRIERS TO REMAIN AT
SEA FOR LONG PERIODS. THE QUANTITIES CARRIED
MAY BE GAUGED BY THIS STOREROOM, WHICH IS
DEVOTED SOLELY TO THE *KITTY HAWK*'S SUGAR
SUPPLY.

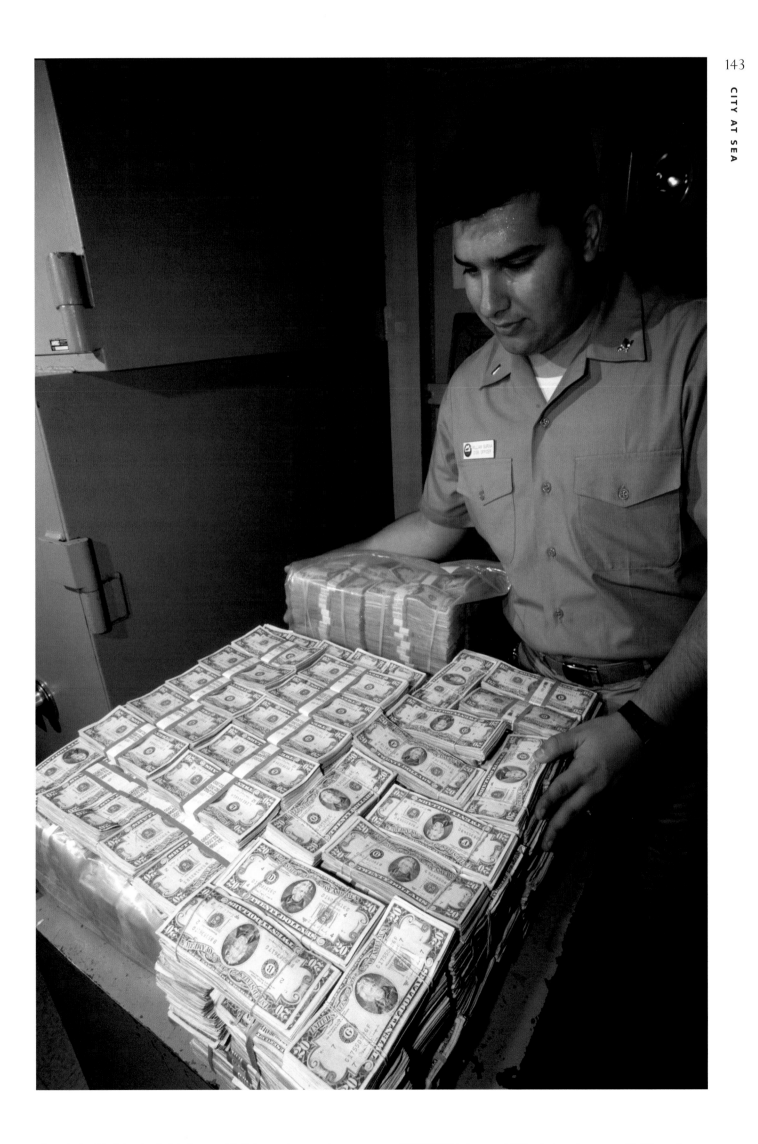

Supply runs the laundry—cleaning and pressing—haircuts, pay, mail and the post office, and the ship's store, where the guys can buy every- thing from toothpaste to clothing, books, magazines—it really is a "mini-mall."

Historically, in the Navy the Captain has always had the "morale" tag. I think our supply guys must run him a close second, and since the poor guy has to be glued to his chair on the bridge for days on end—

well, many in the crew will see more of our "morale servers" on a daily basis. From hamburgers to cheaper rental cars on the beach, we work the morale thing in the Supply Department. MWR—Morale, Welfare, and Recreation—is one of our biggest items. The MWR fund receives money from the central Navy fund, and our retail sales from our ship's store are a big input. Look—you see those soda machines and the video games that are crowded with people most of the time? Sailors play or drink for quarters. In one five-month period the soda machines made us over $320,000 and the games over $100,000—in quarters, yet! Over the same period our retail sales were well over $2 million! Our MWR fund pays for a lot of equipment for our workout rooms, which are heavily used. They make it possible for our sailors to get a lower-cost hotel room or to take great tours when we visit foreign ports—all organized and supervised so that it's an educational experience. At intervals, we throw a big ship's party or picnic for the crew and their dependents: we hire out a big hotel, have well-catered meals, and charge the younger fellows about five dollars, the senior ones seven to ten dollars—the rest coming from your friendly MWR! Fishing trips, ski trips, golf equipment, and reduced fees—it's all a part of making a sailor feel that what he does is appreciated, and that the Navy cares! And not on taxpayers' dollars!

MESS HALL CHIEF PETTY OFFICER

We teach all the food-service personnel that it doesn't take any longer to do the job right. You can dish up a ladle of gray-looking beans, some fatty meat, canned vegetables that are just heated up, and open a can of sickening-sweet canned peaches for dessert, and some people call it food. We don't! Sailors and tastes have changed over the years. Twenty years ago when I was a "boot," we wanted steak, roast beef, spuds, gravy—solid farm stuff. Now these kids think the top thing is hamburgers—"sliders"! We're going to put out a tempting menu, make it look and taste good, make sure the sailors know what the calorie count is, and we'll do our best to reduce the fat content of our balanced menus.

We are very, very conscious of bacteria and the ways they can make a crew sick. At every level our people are taught cleanliness and awareness of the danger of any infection. If one of our personnel gets a cut on his hand, he's off food preparation! A touch of staph could lay the crew out, and what good is a carrier with everyone in a bunk? Hygiene lectures are mandatory, as are the inspections by our Medical Department.

SHIPS' STORES PROVIDE A VARIETY OF READING MATERIALS, CLOTHING, PERSONAL ITEMS, AND ORDERING SERVICES FOR THE CREWS. THE PROCEEDS OF THIS "MINI MALL" IN PART FINANCE THE SHIPS' RECREATIONAL AND WELFARE ACTIVITIES.

LEFT, MASSIVE QUANTITIES OF STEWS,

SAUCES, AND VEGETABLES REQUIRE GIANT-

SIZED KETTLES.

FOOD-SERVICE PERSONNEL DISH UP MEALS

IN THE SERVING LINE TO THE HUNGRY CREW

OF THE *KITTY HAWK.*

See that cook over there? That guy with the real chef's hat on? Well, you know we wouldn't permit one of our guys to grow hair and sideburns like that! He's a real chef, a civilian! He and a few other top chefs from town are riding us for some months, even going to the Med with us—and they're teaching our mess specialists the real scoop on how to fix food not just fancy but the most tasty. Taxpayer money isn't used—they're paid out of nonappropriated funds, our MWR funds. We really surprise our shipmates with some of the treats they cook and teach us to fix. They've caught our spirit and really have become like crew!

We're competing for—and I think we'll win it—the Ney Award for the best food service among the large ships of the fleet. It's a huge incentive, and the competition and judging are tough! Everything counts, including presentation, whether it looks appetizing or not—that's why we decorate all the serving platters with flowers carved out of vegetables, and why we have lots of parsley, celery, and those things to give the food color appeal. Nutrition: they look hard at the fat content, and the balance of mineral-providing foods. Cleanliness, preparation, and taste count lots—and I admit, so does our lobbying! We make sure, from the Captain and XO on down, that every visitor knows we're in the lead, and that they see our food-service lines and how pretty the food is, and how squared away the food servers are. It's a full crew effort.

Now, I want you to see a real team in action! You've seen our different mess halls and wardrooms, and how we're on the "go" around-the-clock. Well, this galley has to get sparkling clean in—get this—twenty minutes! All this space, and all of those steam kettles, the decks, the utensils—because in twenty-one minutes we have another chow-down. Here we go. I have one hundred—count 'em if you want—one hundred food-service guys in this space, elbow to elbow, boiling water, mops sloshing down all the decks, those cooks steaming the kettles . . . Watch out! Each guy has his territory and is going at it, and he'll swab you down if you stand still. Let's step out into the passageway and watch for a minute—I really am proud of these guys and their work habits! It might seem like a thankless job, but they do it and—see—they can even laugh about it!

POSTAL CLERK

"Mail call! Mail call!" That's been a very, very welcome word for soldiers and sailors ever since there was a military! That's our job—mail. Or put another way—we pack and unpack "morale"! If you've ever been away from home, like deployed to the Far East or the Med for months, you can really appreciate those letters from home, and you really do enjoy writing them—but *getting* is best! When we've been out a while, and that COD comes aboard, you can feel anticipation all

ABOVE, COD AIRCRAFT PERFORM THE VITAL ROLE OF SUPPORTING CARRIERS FROM ASHORE, AND COD SQUADRONS FEATURE A NUMBER OF WOMEN PILOTS AND CREW MEMBERS. THIS LOADMASTER, RESPONSIBLE FOR THE PROPER LOADING AND STOWAGE OF CARGO, ALSO RECEIVES GOOD-NATURED JIBES FROM MALE CREW MEMBERS, AS NOTED ON HER NAME PATCH.

OPPOSITE, A COD AIRCRAFT BRINGS SMILES TO THE CREW AS A LARGE NUMBER OF ORANGE MAIL SACKS ARE UNLOADED.

THE POSTAL CLERKS IN THE
GEORGE WASHINGTON'S
POST OFFICE HAVE THE BUSY
TASK OF SORTING MAIL BY
DIVISIONS FOR PICKUP. FRE-
QUENTLY, WHEN THE MAIL
LOAD IS VERY HIGH, WILL-
ING VOLUNTEERS FROM
VARIOUS DIVISIONS CROWD
IN TO ASSIST IN THE DISTRI-
BUTION OF THE MORALE-
RAISING WORDS FROM
HOME.

over the place. Let me tell you, as much as we appreciate having VIPs on board to show off the ship and what we do, we get a sinking feeling when we've been out a while and we see the COD trap and see a spare jet engine in the cargo bay or a bunch of passengers get out. We know that baby can only carry eight thousand pounds, and two-hundred-pound guys take up weight that could have been letters from Mama! Each one means a lot of one-ounce letters, my man!

When that COD comes aboard with mail in those *lovely, lovely* orange bags, our entire mail gang gets busy. We move it from the flight deck down to the hangar deck and to the post office, where it's sorted by our postal clerks into bags by the various departments and divisions. We separate out the official boxes, spare parts and supplies, and official letters from "the good stuff" and try to get the mail in the crew's hands with as little delay as possible. Sometimes the mail load is so heavy that we have to get help from a special working party and volunteers—they aren't hard to get!

Let me give you some numbers. During our last six-month deployment we handled *360,000 pounds of incoming mail*—what's that, about sixty to seventy pounds per man?—and we shipped off 150,000 pounds. Like I said, "getting" is best!

DECK PETTY OFFICER

I'm a standard Mark 1 boatswain's mate, and I'm in charge of a gang in the Deck Department. I'm not a specialized boatswain—not air—just a "general service," Mark 1 type that goes back to the old, "Old Navy"—just like old sergeants in the Army! When you hear the boatswain's pipe sounding off, that's me or another like me. We have seamen under us who are the line handlers when we're mooring or getting under way, handling the lines to the tugs. We put them to work scraping rust and painting, and we're responsible for handling the anchor when we're in channels or going into port. Our big boss is that lieutenant commander you see over there—the First Lieutenant—he keeps about 150 of us busy with always training and cleaning, keeping the ship's boats in 4.0 shape and running the boats when we're at anchor. When you get up to the forecastle, take a good look at how well painted the anchor chains are, and look at yourself in the brightwork—the brass—like a mirror! It makes a clean place for Sunday church services.

We really get a workout during UNREP, when we go alongside a supply ship or tanker for stores or fuel. We "mule-haul" all of the lines and hoses that go over on the booms, and they always end up with an "emergency breakaway" to keep us on our toes. Here's an example of how much we handle in one of those things: in just one we took aboard 230 pallets with more than 340,000 pounds!

ENACTING A TRADITION OF THE OLD NAVY, A BOATSWAIN'S MATE USES THE TRADITIONAL BOS'N'S PIPE TO ANNOUNCE THE ARRIVAL OF A VISITING DIGNITARY ON THE USS *EISENHOWER*.

MARINE

This isn't really what I joined the Marines for, but I'm a marine, I follow orders and do what I'm told. I hope that I get orders to a regular Marine job after a year—I really don't cut it with this big-ship stuff and these tons of people. There are twenty-six of us on board—it used to be eighty or so, but with the changes in weapons, that's been cut. We have a Marine captain commanding the detachment, and he's 100 percent Marine—so's the gunny. We talk like marines, keep our spaces squared away like marines, do PT like marines—oh, do we ever do PT—and train like marines.

We have quick-reaction teams that can respond to all sorts of emergencies that require our use of small arms for many reasons—say, someone tries to break into a cash machine or a safe. We're trained and we practice as a team to conduct extraction of personnel or insertion of our guys: for example, if we had to board another ship to put down a problem—terrorists—whatever. We practice "fast rope" a lot, jumping out of hovering helos from forty to sixty feet above the flight deck, using foot brakes to slow our way down the rope. We have small-arms firing fairly often, shooting at targets on the edge of the deck, and have a lot of fun letting members of the ship's company try their hand with all the weapons. It's even more fun when they try the fast rope or rappeling by the elevators—it takes guts the first time!

A couple of our marines work as captain's orderlies, same as the old days. That's a hard-working, full-time job, and they really have to learn their way about the ship, seeing as how they have to go with the Captain wherever he goes, and he goes everywhere—from steering aft to the pump room, the brig, MarDet [Marine detachment spaces], voids—I mean everywhere! They get a break though—they miss out on a lot of the gunny's meetings and eating-out sessions—you know, the "semper fi" stuff—and a lot of PT!

CHAPLAIN

We have three chaplains assigned to the ship in what is called the Command Religious Ministries Department (CRMD). We also have a number of crew members who are assigned to us on a temporary-duty basis, and then have men of a special Navy rating, religious program (RP) petty officers, who work full time and overtime setting up and administering our many programs. Modern high-tech hasn't done away with the pains of separation from family during cruises and six-month deployment, although it can and does help in many ways. For example, carriers have much better mail capability than other ships because of the COD flights, and we have the ability with radio and satellite to make telephonic connection if necessary.

We have more than eighty different gatherings a week for fellow-

FOLLOWING PAGE, **THE USS *SARATOGA* TAKES ON JET FUEL FROM THE OILER *MONONGAHELA* DURING AN UNDERWAY REPLENISHMENT OPERATION IN THE ATLANTIC.**

ship, in every case a result of an expressed desire by somebody to worship in that fashion. At sea, every day, an average of twelve services are held—sometimes several simultaneously. While many of these are Judeo-Christian, we've recently begun services with a Native American lay leader. In our regular services our attendance isn't always overwhelming: for many, it's hard to break away from work and rest routines, but you might say we do have some real "hard core" congregations.

Aside from the religious services, we manage the library—which is extremely popular—and the crew's lounge. The wait to use one of the five Sprint phones in the library assures some fair amount of traffic our way!

One thing that helps a man keep in touch with his family is a program in which one can choose from a huge selection of children's books and tape-record Dad reading a story for the kids back home. Another is our providing a number of VCR-TVs to view home movies in private. We also manage the ship's branch of the Navy Relief Society and can grant no-interest loans during emergencies, or work with the Red Cross during a personal emergency.

The old maxim "tell it to the chaplain" hasn't disappeared, either. We're available around-the-clock for pastoral counseling, and as sophisticated as young people these days seem to be, there is still a need for an outlet where a person can discuss personal matters and problems with confidentiality and not have to worry about his problem being broadcast on the 1-MC. You might be surprised that those who seek counsel are not just the young and lonely, but also sometimes fall in the senior or leader categories. We are here to listen and to help, and if someone has a suggestion for improving things, they need only stop by or pick up the closest ship's internal telephone. Just dial 7-GOD!

NURSE

I guess we're not a lot different from other carriers. I just like to think that we may do it a teeny bit better. We have an absolutely super Medical and Dental Department. A lot of people might think that we'd have to transfer a surgery case ashore—not so! Our top doctors are fully board-certified surgeons, capable of doing whatever surgeons do in the biggest and finest hospitals. No, we don't have an Ob-Gyn, but a proctologist is a possibility! True, if someone blows out a knee and needs reconstructive orthopedic surgery, we'd COD him ashore, and there are a number of cases when we're deployed that we send ashore because we judge it may be best. But for general surgery, we do it. In fact, I'd prefer the cleanliness and attention we have here to just about any hospital you name. A patient is far less likely to get staph infection or other complications. We have a full-up X-ray capability, a lab that

OPPOSITE, **THE MARINE DETACHMENT PRACTICES A "FAST ROPE" EVOLUTION, SLIDING FROM A HELICOPTER TO THE FLIGHT DECK OF THE** *KITTY HAWK* **IN REALISTIC SIMULATION OF THE INSERTION OF RESCUERS OR INFANTRY SUPPORT.**

PREVIOUS PAGE, **A MARINE CAPTAIN LEADS THE MARINE DETACHMENT ON A LONG JOG AROUND THE** *KITTY HAWK'S* **FLIGHT DECK ON A SUNDAY DAWN, PASSING THE BACKDROP OF F/A-18 HORNETS.**

carries out tens of thousands of procedures a year, and we can make glasses for our sailors.

Last week we had two appendectomies; that patient in the far bunk was a hernia case. Neither too unusual. The man in the cast from toe to hip slipped in oil on the flight deck and tore up ligaments; that one getting the intravenous solution has pneumonia and is improving OK. In that bunk is our training and teaching dummy—we work out our young hospitalmen with it. Always training!

I don't work in Dental, but I can vouch for their work based on my own problems. They're good, and they have plenty of work with the young sailors we have here. Even though they get a great going over in recruit command, they develop lots of cavities—too much sweet stuff and too many soft drinks!

Let me give you a few boring statistics on our last six-month deployment. Over 10,000 sick-call visits—fifty or sixty a day; 24,000 prescriptions; 310 surgery cases; 30,000 plus lab procedures. We medevac'ed fifty some to shore. Thank God that we've had little of the big, tragic things that we train for all the time!

SEAMAN

I come from Hastings, Nebraska—a small place compared to Norfolk. No, I never in my life saw an ocean or even any water bigger than a farm pond, and I guess I couldn't live farther from the ocean anywhere in the U.S.—so I don't know why I picked the Navy, except the thought of living in muddy trenches made me think of hog wallows. The Navy's a pretty clean life. I've only been aboard three months, so maybe I'll get used to it, but it's hard to sleep with all the noise of the planes and cats, and it's hard to find a place where you aren't crowded with people. Even going to the weight room after midnight, there are people waiting to get in.

I do miss home and my family—longest I was ever away was a two-week camp. Now it's coming to hunting season, the best time of the year at home, and I'd sure like to be there! Maybe after a while I can get to be a coxswain of a boat, which would be fun. I look forward to our deployment to the Med—the talk of visiting foreign countries was one of the things that I liked when the recruiters talked to us. Right now I came up here to the flight deck to feel the sun and get off to myself a little, and think of my girl. It's quiet for a bit. That ocean is so blue. It's so big—nothing but water all around!

WIFE, AWAITING SHIP AFTER DEPLOYMENT

I don't care if it rains one inch or twenty, no little bit of rain is going to dampen *our* ardor! We've all been waiting six months for this day!

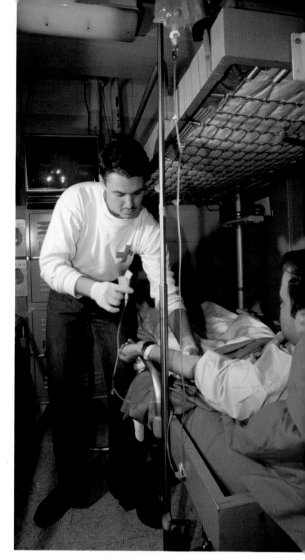

ABOVE, A HOSPITALMAN TREATS A PNEUMONIA PATIENT IN THE VERY WELL EQUIPPED DISPENSARY OF THE *KITTY HAWK*.

OPPOSITE, TOP, A DENTIST TREATS A *KITTY HAWK* SAILOR. *BELOW*, A CATHOLIC CHAPLAIN HOLDS SERVICE FOR "RAINBOW-HUED" SAILORS IN ONE CHAPEL OF THE USS *GEORGE WASHINGTON*.

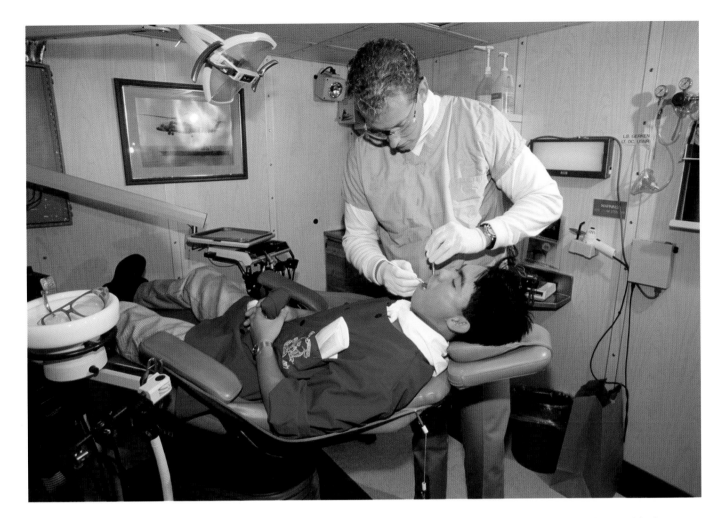

Look, that kid walking in the puddle is in over his shoes! There must be two thousand brand-new dresses or suits getting ruined by the rain. The smart ones are those young girlfriends who stick to their Levis, but a lot of us older wives feel we need everything we can get to feel we're keeping our edge! Lots of parents here, older folks taking chances on pneumonia. And those new babies! You know, the new fathers who haven't seen their babies get to go off first—that tent over there is for the new ones.

This is our third six-month deployment—and I hate them! They are our hell on earth! The Navy does everything they can to help us, but there's no substitute for a husband and father at home. Our kids take their dad as a real novelty for the first month back. Later, if he tries to correct them, they come to me and ask, "Do I have to, Mom?" It's tough on marriages. Sometimes I have to agree with my mother—she's a Navy wife. She says the Navy was better when there were fewer married couples. But she thinks we've been spoiled by all the help we get and with all the programs. I don't! Still, we have lots of problems and divorces—two men who work for my husband are getting them. I think we probably have no more than our civilian friends who we're in church with. The whole world is kinda screwed up, don't you think? Gotta go get my two kids and move up the wharf—looking for a long, tall "string bean" who's gotta take us to dinner tonight—-after we get on dry clothes!

A LONELY YOUNG SEAMAN FINDS A MOMENT OF QUIET ON THE STERN OF THE USS *GEORGE WASHINGTON*, GAZING OUT AT THE VASTNESS OF THE ATLANTIC OCEAN DURING A LULL IN FLIGHT OPERATIONS.

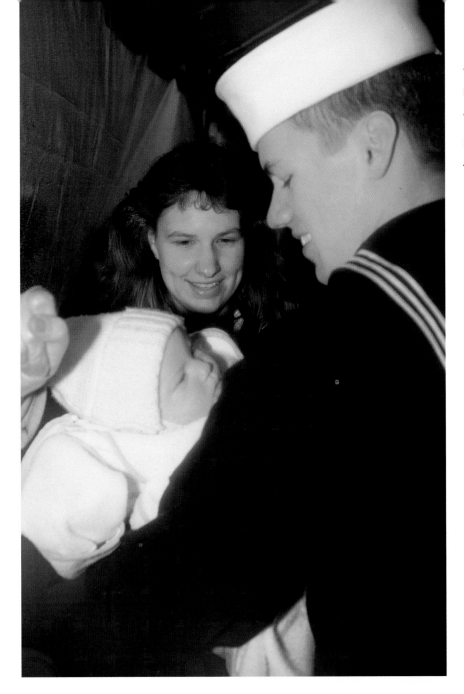

LEFT, FIRST OFF, BY TRADITION, ARE THE NEW FATHERS WHOSE BABIES WERE BORN WHILE THEY WERE AWAY. A SPECIAL TENT PROTECTS THE COUPLES AND BABIES FROM THE WEATHER.

DEPENDENTS, RELATIVES, AND FRIENDS BRAVE HEAVY RAINS TO GREET THE USS *AMERICA* AND ITS CREW UPON ITS RETURN FROM A SIX-MONTH MEDITERRANEAN DEPLOYMENT.

ABOUT THE AUTHORS

Yogi Kaufman, more formally known as Vice Admiral Robert Y. Kaufman, USN (Ret.), is a veteran submariner whose thirty-eight-year naval career embraced both diesel and nuclear submarines. A graduate of the U.S. Naval Academy, he served as executive officer of the nuclear-powered *Seawolf* and commanded the diesel sub *Cavalla* and nuclear attack sub *Scorpion*. After heading the nuclear-power training unit in Idaho, he commissioned the last Polaris submarine, *Will Rogers*. He subsequently served on a panel that determined the characteristics of the *Los Angeles* class and played a leading role in the development of the Trident system. Since retiring from the Navy, he has become a professional photographer whose work is published worldwide.

Steve Kaufman is one of the country's foremost outdoor and wildlife photographers and enjoys the distinction of having his father, Yogi Kaufman, follow in his footsteps. A graduate of the University of Maryland and former National Park Service ranger, he has completed numerous assignments for National Geographic books and *Traveler* magazine, and his photographs of Australia, New Zealand, Africa, Greece, the Sinai and Negev deserts, Siberia, and Alaska appear in publications worldwide. *City at Sea* is his fourth collaboration with his father. Their previous books are two books on submarines, *Sharks of Steel* and *Silent Chase,* and a wildlife/scenic book, *Untamed Alaska.*

The **Naval Institute Press** is the book-publishing arm of the U.S. Naval Institute, a private, nonprofit society for sea service professionals and others who share an interest in naval and maritime affairs. Established in 1873 at the U.S. Naval Academy in Annapolis, Maryland, where its offices remain, today the Naval Institute has more than 100,000 members worldwide.

Members of the Naval Institute receive the influential monthly magazine *Proceedings* and discounts on fine nautical prints and on ship and aircraft photos. They also have access to the transcripts of the Institute's Oral History Program and get discounted admission to any of the Institute-sponsored seminars offered around the country.

The Naval Institute also publishes *Naval History* magazine. This colorful bimonthly is filled with entertaining and thought-provoking articles, first-person reminiscences, and dramatic art and photography. Members receive a discount on *Naval History* subscriptions.

The Naval Institute's book-publishing program, begun in 1898 with basic guides to naval practices, has broadened its scope in recent years to include books of more general interest. Now the Naval Institute Press publishes more than seventy titles each year, ranging from how-to books on boating and navigation to battle histories, biographies, ship and aircraft guides, and novels. Institute members receive discounts on the Press's nearly 400 books in print.

For a free catalog describing Naval Institute Press books currently available, and for further information about subscribing to *Naval History* magazine or about joining the U.S. Naval Institute, please write to:

Membership & Communications Department
U.S. NAVAL INSTITUTE
118 Maryland Avenue
Annapolis, Maryland 21402-5035

Or call, toll-free, (800) 233-USNI.

THE NAVAL INSTITUTE PRESS

CITY AT SEA

Designed and set in Adobe Perpetua, Syntax, and Agfa Ironmonger
by Pamela Lewis Schnitter

Printed on 80-lb. Productolith Gloss Text
by Schmitz Press, Sparks, Maryland

Bound in Holliston Crown Linen with
Permalin endsheets
by American Trade Bindery